The Essential Guide to Apartment Living in Ireland

Robert Gogan

MI Publications

© Robert Gogan 2008

Published by
Music Ireland Publications
Achill Island
Co. Mayo

All rights reserved
No part of this publication may be copied, reproduced,
transmitted in any form or by any means or introduced into a retrieval system without
permission of the copyright owner and the publishers of this book.

Cover designed by Ed McGinley, MGA Design Studios, Dublin.

Printed by Colorman, Dublin

Author's Note

Living in an apartment or private 'gated' development is rapidly becoming the new lifestyle in Ireland's towns and cities, where land is scarce and conventional houses are too expensive. It's the best way to get on the property ladder and perhaps 'trade up' as your financial position improves.

So you make a decision to buy an apartment to live in.

Or maybe you decide to make an investment and buy an apartment to rent out.

Or perhaps you buy a house in one of the new private 'gated' developments located in quiet corners of our towns and cities.

One way or the other, you now discover that you're a member of a limited liability company called a Management Company and there are budgets and Annual General Meetings to deal with, not to mention Service Charges, Managing Agents and Sinking Funds. And perhaps you've got neighbours causing problems and you don't know what to do about it. The chances are that you're confused and frustrated at what's going on but there doesn't appear to be anybody to turn to for answers and clarifications.

Nobody explained any of this to you when you were buying your property.

I hope that this book will solve that problem for you.

From its uncertain and cautious beginnings, apartment living has evolved to the extent that it's estimated that about 500,000 people now live in such environments. Over 20% of all housing units built in Ireland each year consist of apartments or managed properties and the percentage is expected to increase in the coming years.

Owning and living in an apartment or private 'gated' development is completely different from standard house ownership in a regular suburban housing estate. There's a complicated financial and legal structure with precise duties and responsibilities attached to such ownership - duties and responsibilities which are enforceable by law.

From my years working as a Managing Agent, I came to one very distinct conclusion - most people who own or live in these types of development have very little understanding of how the 'system' operates. This ranged from the directors of the various Management Companies - who have a fundamental legal duty to know what they're doing - down to the individual owners who feel they've no control over their situation.

Although living in a private 'gated' development is somewhat different to living in an apartment development, many of the issues concerning administration, costs and control are relevant to both. I refer throughout the book to 'apartment developments' and this should be taken as also referring to private 'gated' developments. Any anomalies or differences between them will be clarified at the end of each chapter.

There's a lot of legal jargon surrounding apartment living in Ireland and I've kept the use of these terms to a minimum in this book. The topic can be complicated enough without the use of unfamiliar technical words and phrases.

I've included, in Appendix A at the back of the book, a glossary of technical words and phrases which frequently arise when discussing the subject of apartment living - together with useful explanations. I've also included in the glossary the substitute words and phrases I use in the body of the book in order to simplify the narrative and make it easier to understand.

Please take a look at Appendix A before reading the main body of the book as it'll help you to understand the various parties and relationships involved in a multi-unit managed development. In particular, check out the definitions of 'Management Company', 'Managing Agent' and 'Board of Directors'. These are the cornerstones of your development and tend to cause a lot of confusion amongst owners.

The management of apartment developments is a complex matter where professional and expert advice should be - but isn't always - sought. The consequences when things go wrong can be far-reaching and costly to all concerned.

Finally, I've used the male 'he' when referring to a developer, owner, Managing Agent, company director, etc. I acknowledge that very many of these individuals are female and that the correct terminology in every instance should be 'he or she'. However, I've restricted the expression to 'he' in this book for the purposes of convenience and brevity. Please accept my regrets if I've offended you by this course of action.

Robert Gogan
January 2008

Acknowledgements

I've consulted with many people in the writing of this book and I'd like to acknowledge the help of Tom English, Health & Safety Consultant for his advice on Health & Safety and Fire precaution matters; Declan Reddy of Declan Reddy Associates for his advice on reinstatement valuations; John McBrearty of Gogan Insurances for clarifying the insurance issues; Brendan Meehan of Meehan & Associates for advice on corporate financial and accountancy matters; and Damien Kelly of Kelly & Griffin, Solicitors for reviewing the legal issues with me. All of these people deal with apartment developments on a regular basis in their professional capacity and their help was invaluable to me.

I'd also like to thank Gerry Tyrrell, Liesl Marcroft, Ted Stapleton, Alan Cooke and Roddy Gallagher for their support in checking the manuscript and Terence O'Sullivan for his suggestions and advice.

Finally, I'd like to thank my wife Anne for her patience, smiles and encouragement during those frustrating days when I wanted to abandon this project and just gaze out the window at the beautiful Achill seascapes - without an apartment block in sight.

R.G.

Bibliography

Consultation Paper - Governance of Apartment Owners' Management Companies no. C/2006/2
  Office of the Director of Corporate Enforcement

A Dubliner's Guide to the Residential Tenancies Act, 2004
  Resident and Tenant Focus Group

Consultation Paper on Multi-unit Developments no. LRC CP 42-2006
  The Law Reform Commission

Successful Apartment Living
  Dublin City Council

Successful Apartment Living part 2
  Dublin City Council

Management Fees and Service Charges Levied on Owners of Property in Multi-unit Dwellings
  National Consumer Agency

Irish Company Law Revision
  Eavan Murphy. Gill & McMillan

Who'd Want to be a Company Director?
  Mark O'Connell. First Law

Guidance of Directors and Senior Managers on their Responsibilities for Workplace Safety and Health
  Health & Safety Authority

Condos, Co-ops and Townhomes
  Mark B. Weiss. Dearborn Trade Publishing

"Refreshingly no-nonsense, the book tackles just about every situation apartment owners will encounter in a clear, accessible style. There are also little nuggets of advice that a less thorough book might overlook."
The Irish Times

"A 'must read' for student estate agents, and property managers. More importantly, if all those who own, or intend to own, an apartment or house with a private 'gated' development in Ireland read this book, there would be no real management crisis, as Gogan clearly demonstrates, most of the problems arise through a lack of knowledge on the part of buyers of the obligations they are committing to."
Alan Cooke, Chief Executive, Irish Auctioneers & Valuers Institute.

"This new book by Robert Gogan explores many of the issues which need to be considered by apartment owners and should make a useful contribution to the ongoing public dialogue."
Evelyn Hanlon, Private Housing Unit, Dublin City Council

Contents

Chapter 1
The Background Basics   **1**
- Renting v Owning   1
- Renting property   2
- Freehold v Leasehold   2
- Private 'gated' developments   4
- Summary   4

Chapter 2
Buying your Apartment - The Procedures   **5**
- Buying a new apartment   5
- A copy of the Lease   6
- Membership or Share Certificate   7
- Who owns what?   7
- You - the Lessee   7
- The developer - the Lessor   7
- The Management Company   8
- The developer's obligations   8
- A Managing Agent is appointed   9
- Some startup problems   10
- Individual apartment problems   13
- First owners' meeting   13
- Ad-hoc owners' committee   13
- The developer hands over   14
- Health & Safety file and Title Deeds   15
- Owners elect Board of Directors   16
- Buying a second-hand apartment   17
- Service Charge arrears   17
- Requisitions on Title   18
- Why such a legal structure?   19
- Private 'gated' developments   19
- Summary   20

Chapter 3
What You Own - The Details   **22**
    Apartment   22
    Car park space   22
    Balcony   23
    Walls   23
    Ceilings and floors   23
    Windows and doors   23
    Glass   23
    Conduits and pipes   24
    Easements   24
    The right to a quiet life   24
    What you don't own   25
    Private 'gated' developments   26
    Summary   26

Chapter 4
Managing Your Development   **27**
    Duties and responsibilities of the Board of
        Directors   28
    Property maintenance   28
    Administration of the Management Company   29
    Legal matters   29
    Accounts control   30
    Insurance matters   31
    The Managing Agent   31
    Do you need a Managing Agent?   31
    The cost   32
    The control   33
    The role of the Managing Agent   33
    Managing Agent's commission on contracts   35
    Dissatisfaction with the Managing Agent   35
    Dismissal of the Managing Agent   36
    Dismissal by the developer   37
    Dismissal by the Board of Directors   38
    Dismissal by the owners   38
    Appointment of a new Managing Agent   38
    Private 'gated' developments   39
    Summary   40

Chapter 5
Living In Your Development   41

Duties and obligations of the owner	42
Pay the rent	42
Pay Service Charges	42
Keep your apartment in good order	42
Domestic waste	42
Use of car space	43
Noise	43
Parties	45
Alarms	46
Persistent alarm problems	47
Aerials and satellite dishes	48
Hanging clothes / shaking mats	48
Birds and domestic pets	48
Signs and advertisements	49
Signs placed in common areas	49
Signs placed in apartment window	49
Wooden floors	50
Letting part only of your premises	51
Single private residence	51
Balconies	51
Structural alterations / exterior decorating	52
Excessive weight / dangerous materials	53
Observe all rules made by Board of Directors	53
Allow access to your apartment	54
Causing general nuisance	55
Indemnify the Management Company	55
Remedies for breaches of the rules	56
Refusal to take action	57
Troublesome neighbours and how to deal with them	57
Tenants	58
Owner-occupiers	59
Contact information	59
Owners	59
Keyholders	61
Tenants	61
A remedy	61
Security	61

Cleaning and landscaping	62
Graffiti	63
Poor water supply	64
Car parking	64
Unallocated spaces	64
Allocated spaces	65
Commercial vehicles	66
Access to car park	66
Marking spaces	66
Space too small	67
Renting out your car space	67
Stolen vehicles	68
Bicycles	68
Lift maintenance contracts	69
Twenty-four hour emergency contacts	69
Damp apartments	70
Structural problems	71
General common area maintenance	71
Private 'gated' developments	71
Summary	72

Chapter 6
Financial Matters 73
Budgets	73
Who decides the budget?	74
Initial budget in a new development	75
The annual budget	76
Budget headings	78
Specific costings - added on or removed	80
Supplemental budget	81
"My Service Charge is too high!"	81
The Sinking Fund	83
Managing Agent's interest in contracts	84
Directors' interest in contracts	85
Payment of the Service Charge	85
Apportionment of the Service Charge	86
If you decide not to pay	87
You can't afford it	87
'A matter of principle'	87
You disagree with the annual budget	88

You just don't like paying bills	89
You don't know how the figures are made up	90
Duty to levy and collect Service Charges	90
Service Charge arrears	91
Administration fees	91
Service Charge Collection Policy	92
Service Charge arrears in a new development	97
Service Charge arrears when selling an apartment	98
Voting rights of owners in arrears	98
The first bank account	99
The control of the bank accounts	100
Sinking Fund account	100
General current account	100
Service Charge apportionment - Years 1 & 2	100
The 'missing' Service Charges	101
Annual accounts and audit	102
Access to company books	103
Directors' access	103
Members' access	103
Private 'gated' developments	103
Summary	104

Chapter 7
Legal Matters — 105

Limited company legal issues	105
Registered office	106
Shortcomings of the company structure	106
Memorandum & Articles of Association	106
Members of the company	107
Register of members	108
Voting at General Meetings	108
The developer's majority vote	109
Company directors	110
Board of Directors	110
Director as 'Fiduciary'	111
Duties of directors	111
Penalties and sanctions against directors	112
Civil liability of directors	113
Powers of directors	115
Appointment, removal and rotation of directors	115

Taking over the Board of Directors	116
Disqualification of directors	117
Should you become a director of the Management Company?	117
Directors' meetings	118
Register of directors and secretaries	119
Company secretary	119
General Meetings of the Management Company	120
Voting at General Meetings with Service Charge arrears	121
Annual General Meeting (AGM)	121
Extraordinary General Meeting (EGM)	122
Who can call an EGM?	122
Amending the Articles of Association	122
Filing of documents	123
Strike-Off	124
Restoration	125
Liability of directors at strike-off	125
Developer's failure to hand over	125
Health & Safety	127
Fire safety	128
Letting your apartment	129
Your responsibilities as landlord	129
Complaint to the Management Company by tenant	130
Private 'gated' developments	130
Summary	131

Chapter 8
Insurance Matters — **133**

Copy of insurance policy	133
Duty to insure	134
Insurance at startup	134
Reinstatement valuation	134
Insurance policies required for an apartment development	135
Block insurance policy	135
Employers' liability insurance	136
Property owners' liability insurance	136
Engineering insurance	137
Individual insurance cover	137

Directors' & Officers' liability insurance	138
Premium payment plans	139
Policy excesses	139
Removal from insurance policy	140
Private 'gated' developments	140
Summary	141

Appendix A — 142
Glossary of terms

Appendix B — 150
Checklist before you buy an apartment

Appendix C — 156
Checklist before appointing a Managing Agent

Appendix D — 158
List of Managing Agent's services

Appendix E — 161
Directors' Management Company information

Appendix F — 162
Sample of House Rules & Emergency Contact Notice

Appendix G — 164
Sample of a 'Service Charge Collection Policy' explanatory document

Appendix H — 167
Useful contacts

Index — 169

Chapter 1

The Background Basics

Even though you've gone through all the legal formalities and paid out a large sum of money for your apartment, you actually don't own the freehold of your unit and you never will.

You're only renting it - in the strictest legal sense.

However, you do have significant property rights over your apartment throughout the term of your Lease, which is usually for a period of five hundred years or more.

But you don't own the freehold.

It's vital that you understand and appreciate this fact because it produces an assortment of legal relationships and everyday situations which represent the difference between owning a house and 'owning' an apartment.

Renting v Owning

There are several basic differences between renting and owning something.

When you own something you can do what you like with it - subject, of course, to the laws of the land. You can paint it, alter it, throw it around, sell it, give it away, etc. After all, not only do you have possession of it but you're also the legal owner of it.

However, if you're renting something the rules are quite different. You'll no doubt have possession of the article and the use of it but that'll only be for a certain period of time. You eventually have to return it to the owner in good condition.

There are usually other conditions attached to renting something. In most cases, the owner can dictate whatever terms he likes before renting the article to you. If it's a car, he might say that no person under the age of twenty-five can drive it or that it can't be taken out of the country, etc. If it's some other piece of equipment, it might be that it must be serviced at regular intervals by competent persons.

And, of course, you must return it to the owner after an agreed period of time, and you must pay the rent.

During the rental term, you'll have possession of the article and the use of it and under normal circumstances, the owner can't interfere with your right of possession and enjoyment of the item.

During the rental period and subject to the rules laid down by the owner, it could be said that you have a 'sort-of ownership' of the goods - but only for a specific period of time.

Renting property

Land, property and buildings are rented out under various arrangements and conditions.

The usual term for renting property in Ireland is 'leasing'. You lease a property for a period of time.

- The rental agreement is called a *lease*.
- The person leasing the land to you - the owner - is called the *lessor*.
- The person taking the lease is called the *lessee*.

Freehold v Leasehold

So where does this leave you with your apartment?

Let's look at the fundamental differences between owning and leasing a property. For the purposes of illustration, I'd like to introduce you to two Irish families – The Freehold Family and the Leasehold Family.

The Freehold Family have just bought a house in a regular suburban housing estate which has been taken in charge by the Local Authority in the usual way.

The Freehold Family own their house - forever. Subject to planning regulations and the laws of the land, they can paint it any colour they wish - inside and outside - partition the rooms inside, set up a business in it, lay down wooden floors, hang out their washing to dry, keep domestic pets, etc. They may decide to maintain it in very good condition or just totally neglect it. It's their decision. After all, they *own* it.

The Leasehold Family, on the other hand, have just leased - ie. rented - a house for a year from its owner. Apart from the fact that the owner - the lessor - has a legal right to inspect the house during the term of the lease, the Leasehold Family will have full and uninterrupted use of the house for the year. The lessor has guaranteed them 'quiet enjoyment' of the property and he can't force them to leave during the lease period - unless they're in breach of the lease terms.

When the period of the lease has finished, the Leasehold Family will deliver possession of the house back to the lessor - the house will *revert back* to the lessor. The lessor, therefore, is said to have a 'reversionary interest' in the house during the period when the Leasehold Family are in possession of it.

There's another fundamental difference between the Leasehold and the Freehold Family. Apart from the fact that the Leasehold Family must pay rent on a regular basis, they'll also have to comply with a set of rules and regulations as set out in their lease, such as keeping the house and gardens in good condition, not doing anything which might affect the insurance on the house, not keeping domestic pets, etc. They also have to hand it back in good condition to the lessor at the end of the lease period.

If they don't keep to these rules, they may find themselves in a considerable amount of trouble if the lessor decides to enforce the terms of the lease.

The whole point of outlining the above is to make it clear to you that when you 'buy' your apartment you actually become a member of the Leasehold Family. You have leased your apartment for a very long period of time and you must comply with a set of rules and regulations.

At the end of the period of your Lease, you must hand your apartment back to the entity that holds the reversionary interest in it and that will be your Management Company. It's the Management Company that owns the freehold of your entire development and consequently the reversionary interest in your apartment.

Your situation, however, is quite different from our Leasehold Family above. Your Lease is probably for a period of between five hundred and a thousand years. The annual rent is most likely to be a nominal amount - about €1 per year - which nobody in all likelihood will bother collecting anyway.

So in reality, you can sleep soundly with the knowledge that under all regular circumstances you *own* your apartment, in the practical sense of the word. Such ownership has been described in many different ways:

- Quasi ownership.
- Equitable ownership.
- Virtual freehold.

For the purposes of simplicity in this book, I'll be referring to the person who bought an apartment as *the owner*, who *owns* his apartment - although, as I've just outlined, that's not true in the strict legal sense.

If you're one of those persons who is worried about what will happen to your apartment when your Lease expires in five or six hundred years time and your apartment reverts back to the Management Company, I'm afraid I can't help you. It's beyond the scope of this book!

Private 'gated' developments

When you buy a house in a private 'gated' development you own the freehold of your house and gardens. You're not leasing it from anybody and you don't pay any rent.

The Local Authority, either by agreement or otherwise, won't be taking the development in charge and therefore the common areas will have to be managed by a Management Company established by the developer at the time of building the houses.

You become a member of the Management Company when you buy your house.

Through your membership of the Management Company, you and your neighbours own the common areas and facilities in your development - roads, footpaths, lighting, drains, etc. The Management Company must arrange for any repairs and replacements of these facilities, the public liability insurance and the management of the refuse collection.

Summary

- ◄ When you buy your apartment you don't buy a freehold interest.
- ◄ You buy a very long leasehold interest which in effect gives you practical ownership of your apartment but not full *legal* ownership.
- ◄ Your ownership will be subject to a set of rules and regulations.
- ◄ Because of the nature of your ownership of your apartment, you're in a completely different legal situation than you would be if you were a freehold owner of a house.
- ◄ You can't buy the freehold of your apartment.
- ◄ In this book, the apartment purchaser will be referred to as *the owner*.
- ◄ In a private 'gated' development, you own the freehold of your house and you *collectively* own the common areas along with all the other house owners in the development.

Chapter 2

Buying Your Apartment - The Procedures

I'll now take you through the transaction and procedures which are involved when you buy a typical apartment in Ireland. Naturally, each apartment development is individual in its own way so some of the procedures may vary a little.

I'll first outline the procedures when buying a new apartment in a new development and will then outline what happens when you buy a second-hand apartment in an older development.

Buying a new apartment

Your journey towards buying your apartment will normally take the following path:

- In the beginning, a developer - who may be an individual but is usually a limited liability company - buys a piece of land and decides to build an apartment development or a mixture of apartments, townhouses and commercial units.
- At this stage he owns the freehold interest in everything – the land, the apartment blocks and the individual apartments, which are still only in the process of being built.
- Sometime during this period, he'll form a Management Company unique to this development - usually a company limited by guarantee - see page 105.
- When setting up the company, he'll nominate his own representatives to act as the subscribers to the Management Company. These subscribers will probably not be apartment owners in the development.
- He'll also nominate the first Board of Directors of the Management Company.
- He'll then arrange for his solicitor to draw up a Lease for each apartment. The terms in each apartment Lease will be pretty much the same except for the purchase price and Service Charge apportionment.
- He'll sign an Agreement between himself and the Management Company in which he promises to transfer all of his interests in the apartment development to the Management

Company for a nominal sum in due course - usually when all the apartments have been sold. In turn, the Management Company agrees to accept the developer's interests and also his obligations under the Lease to manage the development. This is called the Management Company Agreement.
- You carry out your own investigations in accordance with the checklist in Appendix B and are satisfied with the results.
- Your solicitor conducts his own enquiries by way of Requisitions on Title and is also satisfied with the results - see page 18.
- You buy one of the apartments. You hand over your hard-earned money, perform a number of legal requirements and sign the Lease.
- You also sign a document to become a member of the Management Company.
- At the closing of the sale you pay an additional sum called a Service Charge. The Service Charge is an amount of money which was calculated by the developer or his Managing Agent and represents your contribution towards the cost of running your apartment development for the initial year.

Congratulations, you're now an apartment owner!

At this stage, there's a little question which needs to be asked -

To what extent during this whole process did you consider who's going to look after your apartment development, how much it's going to cost to run it, and who's going to pay for it?

You should have been satisfied with the answer to that question before you signed on the dotted line.

A copy of the Lease

You should insist on getting a copy of your Lease from your solicitor before he lodges it with your lending institution. Strike while the iron is hot and insist on a copy of it at sale closing - it'll be right in front of you because you've just signed it.

Some solicitors might tell you that it's part of the Title Documents and full of legal jargon and that you don't need it. That's not true. Although there's a lot of legal jargon in it, there are parts of it - the calculation and payment method for your Service Charges, your duties and obligations, the Management Company's and developer's duties and obligations - which are most relevant to you and are very readable.

The Lease is your rule book and Bible. You should have a copy of it and you're entitled to it.

Membership or Share Certificate

You should also insist on getting your Membership Certificate or Share Certificate depending on the type of Management Company involved. This may not be available at the closing of the sale but you should continue to chase your solicitor for it until you receive it.

Who owns what?

You – the Lessee

You're now a Lessee. You own a leasehold interest in your apartment - the uninterrupted use and enjoyment of your apartment for several hundreds of years together with various subsidiary rights:

- The right to travel through the common areas of your development to get to your apartment.
- The right to be connected to the common electrical and plumbing installations in your development.
- The right to use the common areas for functional or recreational purposes - lifts, bike sheds, bin stores, common area seating, etc.
- The right to benefit from the proper enforcement of the House Rules which prohibit certain anti-social behaviour.
- The right to benefit from the covenants - the promises in the Lease - made by the developer and Management Company in relation to the proper maintenance and management of your development.

As a Lessee, you're also a member of the Management Company – you're obliged to become one under the terms of your Lease.

As a Lessee and member of the Management Company, you also have a set of covenants - duties and obligations - which you must adhere to throughout the period of your Lease - see chapter 5.

The developer – the Lessor

In your Lease, the developer is the Lessor. He's the person or company who has leased your apartment to you for several hundreds of years, for which you paid the purchase price.

At this stage, the developer owns the freehold of your entire development - all of the apartments and the common areas.

The common areas consist of all those parts of your development which can be used by more than one of the apartment owners – ie. the land surrounding the apartment buildings, the entrance lobbies, hallways, gardens, bin stores, bike sheds, lifts, the roof, etc. When you bought your apartment from the developer, he didn't sell any of these things to you – he only gave you the right to use or enjoy them.

The developer also owns the reversionary interest in all of the individual apartments, including yours. He is, in strict legal terms, your landlord.

The Management Company

The Management Company, of which you are now a member, owns nothing. It has two functions at this stage:

- To participate in the signing of every Lease and promising, in it, to take over the developer's interests and obligations when he decides to transfer them.
- To ensure that the company itself is in full compliance with company law regulations.

The developer's obligations

In return for your purchase money, the developer hasn't only given you the various property rights outlined above. He has also given you certain legal covenants or guarantees.

Apart from building your apartment to the specifications and designs originally supplied to you, the developer also has a list of other duties and obligations to perform under the terms of the Lease:

- To keep your development adequately insured.
- To maintain the common areas and utilities of your development in good condition.
- To administer all legal and financial aspects of the Management Company.
- To complete the Management Company Agreement and hand over his legal interests and responsibilities in your development to the Management Company at an appropriate time.

As you can imagine, most developers have little or no interest in taking on these responsibilities and managing your development themselves. Therefore, in the vast majority of cases, the developer will engage the services of a Managing Agent to look after these duties and obligations, *but only in relation to his covenant to manage the development under the terms of the Lease.*

Every apartment Lease contains a clause giving the developer the right to appoint a Managing Agent in this manner.

A Managing Agent is appointed

A Managing Agent is appointed by the developer:
- To manage and maintain your development.
- To administer the Management Company's accounts and legal responsibilities.

At this stage, the Managing Agent is carrying out these functions on behalf of the developer.

A Managing Agent is sometimes appointed very early on in the initial stages of an apartment project. This can be very beneficial both to the developer and to future owners of apartments, as the Managing Agent is then in a position to advise on various practical management issues in relation to the development, for example the location and size of bin stores and bike sheds and the most suitable type of security entrance systems to use - keypad, keys or swipe cards.

The Managing Agent can also calculate and estimate the annual budget for the preliminary years and advise the developer as to the appropriate amount of the initial Service Charge for each apartment. Unfortunately, developers don't always take this advice on board.

Sometimes, however, the Managing Agent is appointed at the last minute just before the first apartment is sold. The first year's budget and Service Charges will already have been decided by the developer. These figures are often unrealistic and the Managing Agent has a difficult task to try to work within them. This invariably leads to problems in subsequent years.

At this stage, the Managing Agent - in theory and in law - is the agent of the developer, but only in relation to the *management obligations* of the developer in the Lease. He isn't an agent of the developer in relation to the completion of the development, the snag lists, the erection of an entrance sign, the completion of landscaping, etc.

We've now reached the following position:
- You've bought your apartment and have moved in - or rented it out to some tenant.
- The developer is selling off the remainder of the apartments and - hopefully - is in the process of completing your development as promised.

- A Managing Agent has probably been appointed and is busy maintaining your development and administering the Management Company.
- Every apartment owner is a member of the Management Company.
- The original nominees of the developer are still the directors of the Management Company.
- Neither the Management Company nor the owners have any legal authority or influence because the developer hasn't yet transferred his interests (his ownership of the common areas and the reversionary interest in the individual apartments) or his responsibilities (the proper management of your development) to the Management Company.
- In certain developments, the owners may be able to exercise some influence in relation to the election of directors at the first Annual General Meeting of the Company - see page 116.

Some startup problems

This will probably be the most difficult and frustrating period for you as an apartment owner in your new development. It's certainly the most difficult time for the Managing Agent.

The difficulties arise when the developer is slow to complete your development and resolve the snagging issues in the common areas.

Apart from the fact that for the first few weeks or months you're possibly living on a 'semi building site' - with the resultant noise, dust and inconvenience - you'll probably also be noticing that there are many problems which are being overlooked. Maybe several of the fittings are hanging off the walls or ceilings in the common areas, some of the doors or windows don't close properly, the car park hasn't been properly marked or numbered, the carpets in the corridors haven't been fitted, the lighting at the entrance hasn't been completed, etc., etc., etc.

Most owners of new apartments, in this all-too-familiar situation, automatically blame the Managing Agent. They contact the Managing Agent in various states of frustration and annoyance and demand that certain works be carried out immediately. Their aggravation increases further when the Managing Agent tells them that there's nothing he can do about it and that it's the developer's responsibility.

Some Managing Agents refuse to deal with owners on these matters and won't respond to their letters and phone calls and this causes yet further frustration and annoyance.

If you find yourself in this position, you'll save yourself much stress and aggravation if you keep the following in mind:

- The Managing Agent isn't responsible to ensure that your development is properly *completed* - this is the responsibility of the developer. Although the Managing Agent is an agent of the developer, it's only in relation to the developer's *management duties and obligations under the terms of the Lease* - to carry out day-to-day cleaning and maintenance of the existing development and to look after legal, financial and administrative issues in relation to the Management Company.
- The Managing Agent has no power or authority to force the developer to resolve any common area snags or problems - he can't act as 'official lobbyist' or representative of the owners, as he has no mandate to do so. Most Managing Agents will try to liaise between owners and the developer in relation to common area snags and will keep the developer informed of owners' complaints. If, as often happens, the developer doesn't take immediate action, there's nothing more the Managing Agent can do about it.

Although, as an apartment owner, I'm sure you don't want to hear this, but at the end of the day it's up to you as an individual to take action. It's you who bought the apartment and if you're unhappy with the developer's responses to your complaints, it's up to you to do something about it. Depending on the problem, you might consider contacting:

- Your solicitor.
- The Local Authority Planning Department - if you feel that the developer is in breach of his Planning Permission.
- The local Fire Officer - if you feel that it's a matter relating to fire safety.
- The Health & Safety Authority - if you feel that the developer's actions or inactions have resulted in an unsafe environment.

Many owners become frustrated and feel that the Managing Agent should himself arrange for these minor problems to be rectified and pay for them out of the Service Charge receipts. It would be very wrong of the Managing Agent to do that - to spend your Service Charge contribution to do work which is the responsibility of the developer.

If the owners' dissatisfaction with the completion of the development stretches over a long period of time, a second problem arises.

When the Managing Agent sends out the Service Charge invoices for Year 2, some owners will take the opportunity to show their dissatisfaction by not paying their Service Charge.

When owners refuse to pay their Service Charge because the developer hasn't completed the snagging, they're actually making a conscious decision not to pay their fair share for:

- The control and removal of their domestic refuse.
- The cleaning of the lobbies and corridors.
- The insurance of the development.
- The maintenance of the landscaping.
- The electricity charges for the common areas.

Many owners in this situation, out of sheer frustration, feel that they can 'get at' the developer by withholding their Service Charge.

The only people you're 'getting at' by withholding your Service Charge are your fellow owners, the Managing Agent....and yourself. Without a steady flow of Service Charge funds into your development, the standard of maintenance and cleaning will inevitably decline and the various services and facilities will eventually be curtailed or withdrawn when the funds dry up - see page 87.

So, what are your options at this stage, to try to get the developer to finish your development and resolve the snagging issues? You've a few alternatives:

- Make a complaint to the official agencies as mentioned above, but only if there are sufficient grounds to do so.
- Try to take control of the Board of Directors at the first Annual General Meeting of the Management Company and then refuse to co-operate with the developer in the sale of any unsold apartments until he addresses the issues. This action will only work under certain circumstances - see page 116 - and I'd suggest taking legal advice before making such a move.
- Ask the Managing Agent to hold a meeting and establish an ad-hoc owners' committee and keep hassling the developer until he takes action. If the Managing Agent refuses to hold such a meeting, send a circular around to all owners and set up your own ad-hoc committee. Organise! You've a better chance of getting the developer to co-operate if there's a collective effort being made to hassle him, rather than a lone voice.

- If the matter is serious enough, you might contemplate, or threaten, legal proceedings against the developer.

Individual apartment problems

You must deal with the developer in relation to any snagging problems within your own apartment - plaster cracks, leaks, electricity problems, etc. The Managing Agent has no responsibility or authority in that area.

First owners' meeting

As soon as is practical after the majority of apartments have been sold, the Managing Agent should arrange an informal meeting of owners:
- To have a general discussion about the development and any management issues.
- To explain the legal structure of the development and the specific role of each sector - Management Company, Managing Agent, developer, owners.
- To elect an ad-hoc owners' committee to represent the owners and liaise with the Managing Agent in day-to-day management issues and, if necessary, to put pressure on the developer to deal with any common area snagging problems.

There's no legal requirement for the Managing Agent to call such a meeting and there's no requirement to advise the developer that such a meeting is being held, although it would be a good idea, in most circumstances, to invite the developer to attend to answer queries from the owners.

If the Managing Agent refuses to hold such a meeting, the owners should arrange to hold one themselves and establish their own committee.

Ad-hoc owners' committee

An ad-hoc owners' committee is one way to alleviate some of the startup frustrations. It also gives the owners an opportunity to have an input, albeit unofficial, into the management of their development during the period while they're waiting for the developer to transfer the development to the Management Company.

It also helps to identify potential future directors of the Management Company when the developer eventually transfers his interests and responsibilities to the Management Company and the owners elect their own Board of Directors.

An owners' committee has no legal standing and therefore can't make any decisions which are binding on either the Managing Agent or the developer. There's also no provision in the Lease for such a committee. However, most Managing Agents and developers will take notice of the opinions and unofficial resolutions passed at these owners' committee meetings, so such committees can have considerable influence on the early management of the development.

From my own experience, it's of great benefit to a Managing Agent to have such a committee, and responsible developers welcome and encourage it.

Managing Agents must take instructions from someone. Technically speaking, under the terms of the Lease, the Managing Agent at this time should be taking his instructions from the developer. However, in many cases, the developer has no interest in the day-to-day management and administration of the development. With such a committee in place, the Managing Agent can work with the owners' representatives, albeit in an unofficial capacity, to deal with many aspects of the management of the development.

This committee can also be the body to put pressure on the developer to carry out work in relation to the proper completion of the development, and, perhaps, to speed up the matter of the transfer of the development to the Management Company.

The developer hands over

The time will come when the developer has sold all of the apartments and has completed the development. As mentioned earlier, this can be a matter of months or even years depending on the developer and the particular development.

He now wants to transfer his interests and responsibilities to the owners. To do this, he completes the Management Company Agreement and sells, for a very nominal sum, all of his interests and ownership of the development to the Management Company. He transfers to the Management Company:

- The reversionary interest which he owns in each individual apartment.
- The freehold ownership of the common areas.
- His duties and responsibilities in relation to the management of the apartment development and the administration of the

Management Company.

Under the terms of the Lease, the Management Company takes over the management and administration obligations of the developer - the 'Lessor's obligations'.

As soon as the legal documents are signed:
- He arranges a General Meeting of the Management Company - usually the first Annual General Meeting.
- His nominee directors resign - if they're still the directors, as will usually be the case.
- The owners elect a Board of Directors from among their own.

Health & Safety file and Title Deeds

At this time, the developer will also hand over the Health & Safety file. This should contain all of the relevant information about the development such as:
- 'As built' drawings of the development and each individual structure.
- Copy of the Planning Permission.
- Architect's Completion Certificate.
- Any relevant Health & Safety, and Fire, Certificates.
- Full information about the plant and equipment under the control of the Board of Directors - instruction booklets, technical data, supplier details, warranty period, etc.

Sometimes this file is handed over at an earlier stage - either to the Management Company's solicitor or the Managing Agent. It's a very important collection of documents and should be kept in a safe place. I know of cases where, owing to a dispute between the Board of Directors and the Managing Agent, the Managing Agent has refused to hand over the Health & Safety file. I would therefore suggest that the original file should be kept, for safe keeping, in the Management Company's solicitor's office and the Managing Agent should receive copies of the documents.

The Title Deeds to the entire development will also be handed over and must be kept in a safe place such as the Management Company's solicitor's office.

The owners are now in charge of the development and the developer plays no further official part in it.

Owners elect Board of Directors

As soon as the developer has transferred his interests and responsibilities to the Management Company, he'll arrange, through the company secretary, to hold a General Meeting of the Management Company. This will usually be the first Annual General Meeting of the Management Company. Under company law, the first Annual General Meeting must take place within eighteen months of the date of incorporation of the company, but this doesn't always happen.

The Articles of Association - see page 106 - will almost certainly state that all company directors must resign at the first Annual General Meeting. They're entitled, however, to put themselves forward for re-election at the meeting.

Therefore, at this first Annual General Meeting, the existing directors - who were nominees of the developer and unlikely to be apartment owners - will resign and the apartment owners will elect their own Board of Directors from among their own.

After the first Annual General Meeting the following should be the position:

- The developer no longer has any legal connection or interest in the development or in your Management Company - unless he's also an apartment owner.
- Your Management Company owns the freehold of the common areas and the reversionary interest in each individual apartment. The Management Company is now, legally, your landlord.
- The apartment owners collectively have control of the Management Company.
- Your Management Company has taken over the responsibilities of the developer in all aspects of the management and administration of the development.

You're now in the position that, when the term of years in your Lease expires, you must hand back your apartment to the Management Company, which now owns the reversionary interest in your apartment. As all of the apartment owners are members of the Management Company, you'll be handing it back to yourself and all of the other owners, collectively.

Now that the developer is gone, one of the first issues the new Board of Directors of the Management Company will have to consider is:

- Should it continue to engage the Managing Agent originally appointed by the developer?

- Should it appoint another Managing Agent?
- Should the directors manage the development themselves without a Managing Agent?

This question is dealt with in detail in chapter 4.

What I've just outlined, is the way the process should evolve in the ideal apartment development. Unfortunately things don't always work out that way.

One of the major issues that arises in many apartment developments in Ireland is the failure, neglect or refusal of the developer to surrender his control over the development and transfer his property interests and management responsibilities to the owners.

This is an extremely frustrating problem for many apartment owners and is discussed at page 125.

Buying a second-hand apartment

When buying a second-hand apartment, the seller assigns his interest in his apartment - the long-term Lease - to you. You become the Lessee and also a member of the Management Company.

As a second-hand apartment will probably be in an older development, it's important that you investigate the 'track record' of the management of the development. There's a list of considerations to check out when buying a new or second-hand apartment and these are outlined in a checklist in Appendix B.

At sale closing, you should also insist on getting a copy of your Lease and your Membership or Share Certificate - see page 6 above.

Service Charge arrears

Service Charge arrears always remain attached to the apartment itself and to the legal owner of the apartment. If you buy a second-hand apartment and there are Service Charge arrears attached to the apartment which aren't paid off at sale closing, you become responsible for those arrears as soon as you become the legal owner of the apartment. When the Board of Directors demands the payment from you, you can't hide behind the fact that it's the previous owner who actually built up the debt.

If you end up in this situation, it's more than likely that your solicitor was negligent in not ensuring that the Service Charge arrears were withheld from the purchase price at the closing of the sale. You should, therefore, contact your solicitor and insist that he pays the arrears and seeks to recover them himself from the previous owner.

Requisitions on Title

As soon as you've paid your deposit to buy an apartment - new or second-hand - your solicitor should send the 'Requisitions on Title' form to the seller's, or developer's, solicitor. Ideally, you should discuss the replies to the Requisitions on Title with him before you sign the contract, but time constraints don't always allow that to happen. You should discuss the matter with your solicitor.

There's a lot of useful information contained in the replies to Requisitions on Title, such as:

- The name of the Management Company.
- A copy of the block insurance policy.
- A copy of the Memorandum and Articles of Association of the Management Company.
- Details of the members' voting rights at meetings - this will also be contained in the Articles of Association.
- The name of the Managing Agent, if any.
- Details of the Managing Agent's annual management fee.
- Details of the Managing Agent's contract, if any.
- Details of the Management Company's accounts for the previous financial year.
- The amount in the Sinking Fund and details of the account in which the Fund is held.
- The amount of the Service Charge payable in relation to the apartment. This will also show if there are any Service Charge arrears attached to the apartment. If there are arrears, the relevant amount should be withheld by your solicitor from the purchase price and paid directly to the Management Company to ensure that there'll be no arrears when you become legal owner of the apartment.
- Details of any anticipated expensive work which is proposed to be carried out in the development in the short to medium term.
- Details of any anticipated claims on the Management Company's funds.

Why such a legal structure?

Apartment owners often ask why we need such a complex structure in order to own and manage an apartment development.

When developers began building apartment blocks in the 1970's, there was no legislation in place to deal specifically with such multi-unit developments. Therefore, the developers and their legal and accounts advisers had to make do with the existing legal frameworks which were available to them at the time.

Using a combination of company law and landlord & tenant law, they formulated structures which fulfilled their requirements.

The shortcomings of this legal structure are now becoming apparent and various government agencies are discussing the need for reform in this sector of the property market, with the introduction of legislation specifically designed for multi-unit developments and the establishment of a dedicated Regulatory Authority.

Private 'gated' developments

There are few differences between a private 'gated' development and an apartment development in the matters outlined above. The main difference is that when you buy your house you're buying a freehold interest in your property.

You also become a member of a Management Company which will own the freehold of the common areas when this is transferred to it by the developer in the same manner as outlined above.

The Management Company then has the responsibility to:
- Manage, maintain and clean the common areas.
- Insure the common areas, particularly for public liability insurance.
- Properly administer the Management Company.
- Comply with the provisions of company law.

The house owners at the first Annual General Meeting of the Management Company will elect a Board of Directors from among their own to undertake these responsibilities on behalf of all of the house owners.

Summary

Timeline of events when buying a new apartment, or a house in a private 'gated' development:

- The developer owns land and builds apartments. At this stage, he owns everything.
- The developer establishes a Management Company using his own nominees as subscribers and directors.
- The developer's solicitor draws up the Title Documents which, in the case of an apartment, will be in the form of a Lease.
- You buy an apartment. The developer gives you a leasehold interest in your apartment. He retains the reversionary interest. In a private 'gated' development you buy the freehold in your house and a collective freehold interest in the common areas.
- You also become a member of the Management Company.
- You pay the initial Service Charge when you buy your unit.
- You're the Lessee of your apartment. You have certain property rights. You also have certain legal obligation under the terms of your Lease.
- The developer is the Lessor and, at this time, your landlord.
- The developer has legal obligations to insure, manage and administer the development. He usually engages a Managing Agent to do this for him.
- The Managing Agent has no mandate or authority to rectify problems in relation to the completion of the development by the developer.
- Some owners refuse to pay the Service Charges in Year 2 because the developer is slow to complete the development. This has no effect on the developer and will only affect the owners as the standard of maintenance and cleanliness in the development drops.
- The Managing Agent usually calls an informal owners' meeting and an ad-hoc committee is elected. This committee has no powers but can act as a collective voice for the owners.
- When all the apartments are sold, the developer transfers his interests and responsibilities in the development to the Management Company by completing the Management Company Agreement.
- The Health & Safety file and Title Deeds are handed over to the Management Company at this time.

- The Management Company takes over the responsibilities of managing the development.
- A formal General Meeting of the Management Company is held - this is usually the first Annual General Meeting.
- The first directors of the Management Company - those appointed by the developer - resign.
- The owners elect a Board of Directors from among their own members.
- The developer is no longer involved in the development.
- If you buy a second-hand apartment, you take an assignment of the Lease and become a member of the Management Company.
- Ideally, you should examine the replies to the Requisitions on Title before you sign the contract.
- If you buy an apartment and discover that there are Service Charge arrears attached to it and the Board of Directors is demanding payment from you, you should insist that your solicitor pays them. He should have cleared the arrears at the closing of the sale.
- Whether you're buying a new or second-hand apartment, you should insist on getting a copy of your Lease, and your Membership or Share Certificate.

Chapter 3

What You Own - The Details

You've now paid the purchase price and you've bought yourself an apartment – or at least you've bought a very long Lease of your apartment.

But what exactly have you bought? What do you now own in the practical sense of the word? To put it another way, what parts of your apartment are you personally responsible for? You may think that this is a very obvious question with an obvious answer, but it's not always as straightforward as it seems.

This is a very important consideration. As time passes and your apartment begins to age a little, it's probable that certain things will start to go wrong or give trouble – water and drainage, electrical, intercom, etc. Obviously there'll be a cost factor involved in having these problems fixed. This is where the 'who owns what' issue becomes very relevant.

If, under the terms of the Lease, you're considered to be the owner of the problem piece of equipment or property, then you'll have to pay for the repairs yourself. If you don't own them and they form part of the common areas or common facilities, the Management Company will have to pay for repairs or replacement.

Your Lease will outline the various parts which make up your individual apartment. You can check out in detail the legal terminology for what you've bought under the section in your Lease which begins with the words "All That And Those….", or under one of the Schedules of the Lease entitled "The Premises".

The extent of what you bought will probably fall into the following categories:

Apartment
This is usually described in the Lease as "the apartment known as Apartment no. x" and it should be identified on an attached map.

Car park space
If you're buying a car parking space, it should also be identified either by a number and/or an outline of a particular space on a map. It's important to note that in some Leases you don't actually buy (or lease) the car park space itself. You only buy a licence to use that specific space for the duration of your apartment Lease. The effect

on your enjoyment and use of it is the same.

In many situations, your apartment Lease may give you the right to park a car in the general car parking area without specifying a particular space - this can be quite a problem if there are more occupiers' cars than spaces available.

Balcony

In many Leases, you don't 'buy' the balcony but merely buy a licence to use it for the duration of your Lease. In those circumstances, the Management Company is usually responsible for its maintenance and upkeep.

Walls

You own, and are responsible for, the parts of the walls facing into your apartment - ie. 'severed medially'. The other half of the wall is owned either by another apartment owner - if there's an apartment on the other side of the wall - or by the Management Company - if the wall forms part of the common areas of the apartment block - such as a corridor, stairwell or exterior wall of the building.

Ceilings and floors

You also own and are responsible for the ceilings and floors of your apartment. This normally includes the joists and beams on which the floors are laid out, but not the joists and beams to which the ceilings are attached. Some Leases limit your ownership and responsibility to the floor and ceiling finishes.

Windows & doors

This can be quite a difficult area in relation to apartment Leases and ownership. There are many Leases which make no mention whatsoever of the windows or the entrance door to your apartment. Some Leases say that you own the entrance door and the interior of your window frames – the Management Company being responsible for the exterior of the window frames. Other Leases state that you're responsible for the entirety of your windows and doors, interior and exterior.

Glass

Apartment Leases, in general, are very clear on this subject. You own and are responsible for both sides of the glass in your windows. But who is responsible for cleaning the exterior of the windows? Most Leases make no mention of this at all. Technically speaking, each owner is responsible for cleaning both sides of the window glass himself, as he owns it. However, the outsides of windows are inaccessible from most apartments. It would, therefore, be necessary for each apartment owner to hire contract cleaners to clean the outsides of their windows if their apartment is above the first floor, as they won't be able to reach them.

As the Board of Directors usually has to engage contract cleaners to clean the exterior of the common area windows on a periodic basis, it makes total sense for these cleaners to clean all the exterior glass while they're on site, and the cost of this to be incorporated into the annual budget.

If some owners are opposed to this idea - particularly those who live on the ground floor - the Board of Directors may not be able to implement the scheme unless the terms of the Lease permit them to do so.

Conduits and pipes

You're also buying – and you therefore own and have a responsibility for – all water tanks, cisterns, radiators, sewers, pipes, conduits, drains, wiring, etc. which specifically serve your apartment alone.

This is the area in which most of the maintenance and repairs need to be carried out and where most of the problems and disputes arise.

There's a widespread belief among apartment owners that if there's any water leak or electrical problem whatsoever in the apartment development, it's the Management Company's responsibility. Not so, I'm afraid.

If the source of the fault is some pipework, drains, wiring, etc. specific to your apartment, not only is it your responsibility to have the fault repaired, but you must also bear the costs.

If you're slow to carry out the repairs or simply refuse to do so, the Management Company can arrange to have the work done and charge you for it.

Easements

You also own, along with all of the above, certain easements. These are better known as rights-of-way, allowing you and your family/acquaintances to use the common areas and allowing you to connect various pipes, sewers and power cables to the common area installations.

The right to a quiet life

You've also bought another right, which you can neither see nor touch - that is the right to 'peaceful and quiet enjoyment' of your property.

In the same manner as you signed your Lease promising to comply with the House Rules, so too did every other owner in your development. Their promise to you to keep to the House Rules is a right which you've bought. You can legally enforce it if necessary.

In most Leases, the Management Company also enters into a covenant to ensure that you'll have quiet enjoyment of your property and to pursue any occupier, on your behalf, who is in breach of the House Rules or any other terms of the Lease.

What you don't own

All the other areas of your apartment development are known as the common areas, 'reserved property' or 'retained lands'.

The common areas and the facilities under the control of the Management Company consist of all of the areas and facilities not under the ownership of any individual apartment owner.

They normally include some or all of the following:
- Lifts.
- Bin stores.
- Bike sheds.
- Stairwells, corridors and interior public areas of the apartment buildings.
- Your car space and the balcony of your apartment. Although you've an exclusive licence to use these areas, you don't own them - they form part of the reserved property, or retained lands, under the Lease.
- All main entrance doors to the apartment buildings and gates into your development.
- All of the exterior areas of your development.
- The roofs of the apartment buildings and the roof spaces.
- All exterior walls and all other walls facing into a common area.
- All other electrical or mechanical installations and fittings not directly connected to your apartment.
- Swimming pools, gyms or playground areas.

The Management Company owns all of the above and is responsible for managing and maintaining these areas and facilities in accordance with the terms of the Lease.

Private 'gated' developments

In relation to a house in a private 'gated' development, you own all of the buildings, walls, pipes, cables, drains, etc. contained within the plot which you've bought. You own them outright - you have a freehold interest. You're therefore responsible for the maintenance and repair of these items.

As the Management Company owns the common areas, you've also bought certain easements, or property rights, the main ones being:

- The right-of-way for yourself and your visitors over the common areas.
- The right to have your cables, water pipes, drains, etc. connected to the common pipes and drains of the Estate.
- The right to peaceful and quiet enjoyment of your property within the development.

Summary

- ◄ When you buy an apartment, or house in a private 'gated' development, you've a responsibility to maintain all items which are specific to your property.
- ◄ Your Title Deeds or Lease will outline in detail the items which you've bought and are therefore your responsibility to maintain.
- ◄ You also have the right to peaceful and quiet enjoyment of your property.
- ◄ The Management Company owns the freehold of the common areas and all the common facilities and is therefore responsible for their maintenance and repair.

Chapter 4

Managing Your Development

The overall management of your development will ultimately rest with the Board of Directors of the Management Company, elected by the owners after the developer has transferred all of his interests and responsibilities in the development.

Throughout this chapter, I use the example of a development where the developer has transferred his interests to the Management Company and therefore no longer plays any management part in the development.

If the developer hasn't yet transferred his interests, you should replace the term 'Board of Directors' with 'developer' throughout this chapter in relation to the maintenance and management of the development.

Until the developer transfers his interests and responsibilities to the Management Company:

- He's responsible for the management and maintenance of your development
- The original directors - nominated by himself - are responsible for all matters relating to the compliance of the company with company law regulations.

When the developer transfers his interests and responsibilities to the Management Company, and his nominee directors resign:

- The new Board of Directors, elected by the owners, takes over responsibility for the management and maintenance of the development, and the legal, accounting and administration of the Management Company. The Board of Directors of the Management Company has this responsibility - *not the owners*. Although you're an owner in the development - and therefore a member of the Management Company - your functions and powers are limited. See chapter 7.

In the majority of developments, a Managing Agent will be engaged - at first by the developer and later by the Board of Directors - to carry out the functions of an agent in the management of the development - see page 31 and Appendices C and D.

Duties and responsibilities of the Board of Directors

The duties and responsibilities of your Board of Directors can be divided into these broad sections:
- The maintenance of the property of your development - repairs, renewals and cleaning.
- The administration of the Management Company and the control of the accounts.
- The enforcement of the House Rules and the other owners' obligations under the Lease.

Every Lease will be a little different in how it handles each of these issues, particularly in the terminology or wording used, but the duties and responsibilities will remain the same.

Property maintenance
- Keep and maintain the common areas in good order and condition. This is a very broad responsibility and requires that the Board of Directors makes arrangements to engage the necessary contractors and caretakers to clean and maintain the common areas. Not only is it responsible for appointing competent contractors, but it's also responsible for supervising the work. The Board of Directors must also satisfy itself that the contractors have adequate insurance cover and comply with all Health & Safety regulations.
- Attend promptly to any problems which arise in the common areas – particularly access, water leaks, electrical and plumbing problems. The Board of Directors should obtain a number of quotations for repair work and ensure that any work is carried out properly.
- Prepare a plan for the periodic maintenance of certain plant and machinery – lifts, water pumps, emergency lighting, fire alarms, fire extinguishers, automatic gates.
- Prepare a plan for the regular control of pests - rats, mice, ants, etc.
- Prepare a plan for the upgrading of the common areas. This plan should include a schedule for the repainting of the common areas, replanting of the landscaped areas, cleaning - inside and outside - of the common area windows and the eventual replacement of common installations - lifts, smoke ventilation systems, CCTV systems, etc. If your Lease says

that you're responsible for certain items - window glass, balcony rails, apartment door, etc. - it may also have a provision that the Board of Directors may, at its discretion, clean and maintain these items and provide for the cost of the work in the annual budget. If the Lease doesn't make this provision, the issue should be discussed with the owners.
- Keep a schedule of all common electrical and mechanical equipment installed, sets of architect's plans and mechanical and electrical drawings of the apartment development - the Health & Safety file. This should include the various commissioning certificates in relation to lifts, fire alarms, water pumps, automatic gates, etc.
- Keep the common areas adequately lighted.
- Control and manage the domestic refuse in the development. This generally extends only to the management of the occupiers' *domestic* refuse and not to such items as old furniture and carpets and the packaging materials which accompany all household and flat-packed goods. It's the responsibility of each owner or occupier to dispose of these themselves. However, your Board of Directors will normally end up having to deal with most of it, because this sort of material inevitably finds its way into the bin stores with no chance of identifying the culprits.
- Prepare a Health & Safety Statement if one is required under the Health & Safety regulations- -see page 127.

Administration of the Management Company

This area of responsibility can be divided into:
- Legal matters.
- Accounts control.
- Insurance matters.

Legal matters

The legal administration of a limited liability company is both complex and highly regulated and is dealt with in detail in chapter 7.

The principal legal responsibilities of the Board of Directors are:
- To arrange and convene all General Meetings of the company in accordance with company law and the Articles of Association of the Management Company.
- To properly maintain the company ledger with accurate records of directors' meetings, resolutions passed, etc.

- To maintain the company registers to record details about company members, directors, directors' interests in other companies, etc.
- To file all company documents, including the Annual Return, in the Companies Office.
- To furnish replies to Requisitions on Title when an owner is selling his apartment and to provide copy documents where necessary.
- To issue a Membership or Share Certificate to new apartment owners.
- To take prompt action, legal and otherwise, when owners or occupiers are in breach of the rules and regulations as set out in the Lease. This particularly includes taking action to recover arrears in Service Charges.

The Board of Directors can fulfil most of its duties if it engages the services of a Managing Agent and a company secretary, and also appoints a solicitor to the Management Company. In these appointments, the Board of Directors has a duty to check that the people or bodies appointed are competent and have adequate professional indemnity insurance and financial bonding where necessary.

Accounts control

The financial aspects of a typical apartment development are dealt with in detail in chapter 6. However, in brief, these are the Board of Director's responsibilities in this area:

- To ensure that proper checks and controls are in place to safeguard the assets of the Management Company.
- To prepare the annual budget, taking into account the expenditure for the previous year and the anticipated expenditure for the forthcoming year.
- To calculate the amount of Service Charge to be paid by each apartment in accordance with the Lease, and to send out a Service Charge invoice to each apartment owner.
- To ensure that the Service Charges are paid by the appropriate date and lodged into the Management Company's bank account.
- To take prompt action to recover all Service Charge arrears and to impose interest, under the terms of the Lease, on all overdue Service Charges.
- To maintain proper books of account in order to determine, at any time, the financial position of the company.

- To make arrangements for the preparation of financial statements and to arrange for the audit of the company's accounts.
- To maintain an adequate Sinking Fund, also known as a Reserve Fund.

Insurance matters

This is a very important area of responsibility for the Board of Directors and is dealt with fully in chapter 8. These are the main obligations in this regard:

- To ensure that the apartment development is adequately insured against the usual insurance risks.
- To supply accurate information to the insurance broker in relation to the valuation of the buildings and equipment in the development.
- To arrange adequate engineering insurance on all lifts and pressure equipment in the development.
- To arrange adequate employers' liability and public liability insurance cover in relation to the development.
- To arrange, where possible, a realistic excess on all claims.
- To attend to all insurance claims.
- Although it's not a legal requirement, the Board of Directors should ensure that there's a Directors' and Officers' liability insurance policy in place to protect the directors against civil claims for negligence.

The legal duties of the Board of Directors in relation to insurance extend only to the degree that it's able to obtain the required insurance cover and make decisions on the excess level.

The Managing Agent

Do you need a Managing Agent?

There's usually a Managing Agent on board when the developer transfers his interests and responsibilities to the Management Company. A decision, therefore, has to be made either to:

- Retain the existing Managing Agent.
- Appoint an alternative Managing Agent.
- Dismiss the Managing Agent and manage the development without one.

It's a very important decision and one which should be considered carefully by the owners and the new Board of Directors of the Management Company. The final decision lies with the directors as they have the ultimate responsibility for the proper management of your development once the developer has gone.

If you examine the various services which are required for the proper management of a development, as outlined in Appendix D, you'll realise that it's not really feasible for a group of unprofessional and inexperienced people to undertake the task in their spare time.

In my opinion, it's not a good idea for owners to manage a development themselves unless:

- It's a very small development.
- There's an eager group of people among the owners with sufficient spare time, knowledge, experience, competence and enthusiasm to be able to deal with all the issues involved.
- These people are prepared to give generously of their time and energy to manage the development.

During my time working as a Managing Agent, I came across many apartment developments which were being managed by the owners themselves without a Managing Agent. In all cases, the directors felt that they were doing a very good job; that there was very little to do; and that their development almost "managed itself". They were only considering engaging a Managing Agent because they wished to retire and no other owners were prepared to take on the responsibility.

On close investigation, I discovered that most of these developments were not being managed properly, with problems such as:

- There were Service Charge arrears and little effort being made to collect them.
- The insurance cover was inadequate.
- The company records in the Companies Office were inaccurate.
- There was a non-existent or very inadequate Sinking Fund.

In all cases, the directors and owners were unaware of the seriousness of these matters and were under the impression that their development was being managed very well.

In my experience, there are two principal reasons why owners are reluctant to engage a Managing Agent:

The cost

The Managing Agent's fee will significantly increase the annual Service Charges and will undoubtedly be one of the larger cost factors in the annual budget. However, a competent Managing

Agent is a valuable asset to an apartment development and can contribute to a reduction in certain costs.

If you feel that the Managing Agent's fees are too high, it's a useful exercise to calculate the fees per apartment. If you then calculate the fees per apartment *per month* you'll probably realise that engaging a Managing Agent is good value for money - provided, of course, that the particular Managing Agent is competent and that the owners are satisfied with the level and quality of service being provided for the management fee.

In smaller apartment developments, the Managing Agent's fee will be greater per apartment than in larger developments. This comes down to the reality of 'economies of scale'.

The control

Some directors are reluctant to engage a Managing Agent because they believe that:

- They're going to lose control of their development.
- The Managing Agent will dismiss the existing cleaners, gardener, etc. and appoint their own contractors.
- The Managing Agent will introduce all sorts of rules and regulations against the wishes of the owners.

The Managing Agent isn't in a position to do any of these things without the consent of the Board of Directors, which represents the owners in this matter. At all times, the Managing Agent is engaged by the Board of Directors and must take his instructions from it. The Management Company directors are in charge of the development and determine how it's to be managed by the Managing Agent.

Having said all of the above, it's only fair for me to add that I'm aware of apartment developments which are being managed by the owners themselves in a highly professional and competent manner. Unfortunately, they're in the minority, but it shows that it can be done without a Managing Agent.

It can't be done, however, without considerable commitment from a number of dedicated owners.

The role of the Managing Agent

The Managing Agent is precisely as described – an *agent* to your Management Company. His function is to act as a servant to your Board of Directors, taking care of the day-to-day issues in relation to the management and administration of the development.

He's not the 'executive manager' of the development. The directors of the Management Company, as representatives of the owners, are the executive managers of the development. They're in charge of the running of the development, and all the responsibilities in that regard rest with them.

The Managing Agent is a 'facilities manager', taking care of the common facilities and services of the development and administering the legal and financial structures of the Management Company. In the course of doing this, the Managing Agent can make certain decisions and take certain actions in relation to the day-to-day running of the development, such as:

- The replacement of locks, glass, bulbs.
- The issuing of letters to owners and occupiers for breaches of the House Rules.
- The appointment of contractors for small and medium repair work.
- The payment of all invoices in relation to the development.

He should be permitted to carry out these functions without having to refer back to the Board of Directors all the time.

It'll always remain the responsibility of the Board of Directors to make all the management decisions in relation to the apartment development. The Board of Directors is under no legal obligation to consult with the owners on any of these matters.

The Managing Agent must take his instructions from the Board of Directors and not the owners.

In many apartment developments, there are half-hearted and disinterested directors who work on the assumption that when they appoint a Managing Agent they can sit back and leave everything to him. They expect him to make all the decisions and not bother them. This can make matters very difficult for a Managing Agent. The Managing Agent needs a strong and energetic Board of Directors so that they can work together to give full effect to the terms of the Lease and properly manage the development.

You should always keep in mind that:

- The Lease and Articles of Association set out, very clearly, the responsibilities of the Management Company as undertaken by its Board of Directors.
- The Board of Directors can delegate routine issues within its responsibility to the Managing Agent.

- Neither the Board of Directors nor the Managing Agent can make decisions or operate outside the powers granted to them under the Lease or Articles of Association of the company.

The role and responsibilities of a Managing Agent in the initial stages of a new development are discussed in chapter 2.

Managing Agent's commission on contracts

In addition to the management fee, some Managing Agents charge a percentage of the contract price for each contract which they negotiate on behalf of the Management Company. The problem here is that they don't always tell the Board of Directors. This is known under various names in the commercial world and the words 'kickback' and 'backhander' come to mind.

The Board of Directors should specifically ask the Managing Agent whether or not he receives any such commission - see Appendix C.

In my opinion, there are several reasons why the directors shouldn't accept this situation:

- It lacks transparency.
- It can lead to the Managing Agent not trying to get the best value contracts for the development - the higher the contract price, the higher his commission.
- The Board of Directors is unaware of the true value of the contracts and therefore can't make comparisons.
- It's almost impossible to calculate the true cost of the Managing Agent in such circumstances.

Dissatisfaction with the Managing Agent

The concept of 'service' is a personal one and acceptable standards can vary considerably between individuals. If you're thinking of buying a particular article, you can look at it, touch it, feel it and then make up your mind and say, "That's what I want" or "I don't want that – it's not good value for money".

However, because you're buying *a service* from a Managing Agent, it's quite different. As you're not buying a physical item, you need to find out from the Managing Agent exactly what level of service he's selling to you.

There are many different attitudes amongst apartment owners to their Managing Agent, among which are:

- The Managing Agent is super. He's efficient and competent and his management fee is reasonable (a rare enough opinion!).
- The Managing Agent's fee is too high.
- The Managing Agent is useless and not doing enough to ensure that the developer completes the development properly.
- The Managing Agent is useless and never has enough staff available to immediately address every issue which arises even if it's not an emergency.
- The Managing Agent never replies to letters or returns phone calls.

Before appointing a new Managing Agent, it should not be a case of the Board of Directors asking:

"What sort of service are you going to provide for us?"

It should be more a question of the Managing Agent asking the Board of Directors:

"What sort of service are you expecting?"

or more to the point:

"What level of service are you prepared to pay for?"

Apartment owners complain bitterly about the fact that their Managing Agent offers a very poor service. "All they do is send out the Service Charge invoices and pay the cleaners and gardener and a few other bits and pieces. And they never return calls!"

In some of these cases, there's a possibility that the Managing Agent's fee is too low and he may be providing a sufficient level of service relative to the management fee he's charging.

In this situation, when the Board of Directors or owners are asked, "Are you prepared to pay more money to get a better service?" the answer is usually, "Definitely not! Our Service Charges are high enough already!"

If you're happy enough that your Managing Agent provides a very basic management service at your development in return for a minimal management fee, then you shouldn't be frustrated or annoyed at the level of service.

Dismissal of the Managing Agent

If the Board of Directors or owners are dissatisfied with the standard of service being provided by their Managing Agent, they can consider dismissing him and appointing a new Managing Agent.

This is quite a major decision and will involve a lot of work for the Board of Directors, so I'd suggest that you first meet with the current Managing Agent and try to sort out the problems.

- Maybe there's a communications breakdown that can be rectified.
- Maybe the employee in the Managing Agent's office who deals with your development is incompetent and the Managing Agent might be prepared to replace him.
- Maybe the management fee is so low that it's impossible to provide the standard of service expected.
- Maybe there's a member of your Board causing so much aggravation to the Managing Agent in an unreasonable manner that he has lost interest in your development.

If, following meetings and discussions, the service is still so poor that you want to replace the Managing Agent, there are different situations to consider. These situations will depend on whether or not there exists a formal written contract with the Managing Agent. If one is in place, the parties would need to examine the terms, particularly those in relation to the termination of the contract.

Dismissal by the developer

The developer is responsible for the Managing Agent if he's still in control of your development. The only influence the owners have in this situation is to make an approach to the developer, either individually or through an ad-hoc committee, and to ask him to replace the Managing Agent.

Sometimes the developer and the Managing Agent are colleagues or 'cronies' and therefore he may refuse to replace him. There's not a lot that the owners can do in those circumstances.

If things get bad enough you could threaten to sue the developer for breach of contract due to the mismanagement of your development. Even though he has appointed a Managing Agent, the developer is still ultimately responsible for the Lessor's duties and obligations under the Lease.

This is quite a radical course of action, but very often the mere threat of legal proceedings can bring the desired result. A bad Managing Agent can be so detrimental to a development that such a course of action may have to be considered.

Dismissal by the Board of Directors

When the development has been handed over to the owners, it's the Board of Directors that is responsible for the hiring and firing of the Managing Agent. The directors must take account of any contractual terms, and work within those terms.

In some developments, the developer will have entered into a long-term written contract with the Managing Agent. The Board of Directors may, therefore, have no choice but to use the Managing Agent for several years, even after the developer has transferred his interests. In those circumstances, and if the matter is serious enough, I'd suggest that the Board of Directors should instruct the Management Company solicitor to carefully examine the contract to see if there's a way out.

Very few of such contracts are water-tight and it's quite probable that there are grounds on which the contract can be terminated - even on the implied term of the contract that the service provided by the Managing Agent should be provided in a competent manner.

Unless provided for in the Lease or the Articles of Association, the Board of Directors need not consult with the owners or take their opinions into account when hiring or firing the Managing Agent, as this is a matter directly relating to the 'business' of the company and the directors are solely responsible for the management of the business of the company.

Dismissal by the owners

Under normal circumstances, there'll be nothing in the Lease or Articles of Association to permit the owners to have any authority in the management of the development and this would also extend to matters relating to the Managing Agent.

However, if the owners so wish, they can amend the Articles of Association and insert a clause to the effect that they can decide at a General Meeting of the company to appoint or dismiss the Managing Agent.

The question of owners' involvement in the day-to-day management of the development through the Articles of Association is discussed on page 122.

Appointment of a new Managing Agent

Considerations to be taken into account when examining the credentials and proposed level of service to be provided by your new Managing Agent are dealt with in Appendices C and D.

Before appointing a new Managing Agent, the Management Company directors need to be clear in their mind about the level of service they want and the level of service which they're prepared to pay for. They should carefully consider:

- The authority and responsibilities which the Managing Agent will have.
- The professional competence of his employees.
- The standard of service to be provided and to be expected.
- Response times and other timescales for action.
- The acceptable lines of reporting and communication.

If you expect a top-class service, it may be a case of having to pay a more realistic management fee.

Private 'gated' developments

There's very little difference between the issues which arise in relation to the management of a private 'gated' development and an apartment development.

The duties and obligations of the Board of Directors of the Management Company still fall into the same three categories:

- The maintenance of the development - repairs, replacements, cleaning and refuse management.
- The administration of the Management Company and the control of the accounts.
- The enforcement of the Estate Rules.

The management input will be less than that for an apartment development. There are no internal areas to be maintained and repaired and less time and energy will be required to enforce the obligations of the house owners - the Estate Rules - as these will be considerably less extensive.

The question of whether or not a private 'gated' development requires the services of a Managing Agent comes down to the same consideration as in an apartment development - is there a sufficient number of owners available who are prepared to donate their time and energy on a voluntary basis to act as directors of the Management Company and manage the development?

Even though the number of issues to be dealt with is smaller, it's easy to underestimate the amount of time and effort required to carry out the functions of the Management Company, even in a private 'gated' development.

The Managing Agent's fee should be considerably less than that required in an apartment development. However, many of the private 'gated' developments would have a smaller number of units than an average apartment development and economies of scale can give the impression that the Service Charges and management fees per house are comparatively high.

Summary

- ◄ The Board of Directors of the Management Company is responsible for the management of the development and it doesn't have to consult with the owners when making management decisions.
- ◄ The management duties fall into three categories: (a) property maintenance and repair, (b) administration and accounts, and (c) enforcement of the House Rules.
- ◄ In apartment developments and private 'gated' developments, a Managing Agent should be engaged unless there's a group of owners who are competent and enthusiastic and who are prepared to act as directors of the Management Company and give freely of their spare time to manage the development.
- ◄ The Managing Agent's function is to take instructions from the Board of Directors and to put into effect the management decisions of the Board.
- ◄ It's not a good idea for the directors to permit the Managing Agent to receive a commission on any contracts negotiated on their behalf.
- ◄ If you feel that the Managing Agent is providing a poor level of service, it may be that the Board of Directors negotiated a management fee that is unrealistic and too low for the level of service expected by the owners.
- ◄ Depending on the situation at the development, the Managing Agent can be dismissed by either the developer, the Board of Directors or the owners.

Chapter 5

Living In Your Development

There are many differences between day-to-day living in an apartment, and living in an ordinary house.

If you live in your own house, you've complete freedom in relation to how you enjoy that facility provided you stay within the law. With an apartment, there are clearly defined regulations as to how you use your living space and the common areas around you. In an apartment development, you're dealing with a lot of very diverse people living in close proximity to each other and in a relatively confined area - there has to be a good deal of co-operation and 'give-and-take' on the part of the owners and occupiers for life to run smoothly.

The rules and regulations as to how you conduct yourself within your apartment development are commonly known as the 'House Rules'. They exist primarily to create a peaceful living environment among the occupiers and to maintain the outward visible aspects of your development as a high-class residential location.

Apart from the House Rules which govern behaviour, there are other regulations by which the owner - as opposed to the occupier - are bound. These regulations exist to ensure the smooth management of the development by the Board of Directors.

The rules are not mere guidelines or suggestions for proper conduct. They're legally binding duties and obligations set out in your Lease. You don't legally own your apartment like you would a house and therefore you don't have complete control over how you use it.

This interdependence becomes more pronounced in apartment developments where there are many owner-landlords and therefore a lot of apartments rented out to tenants. Tenants generally tend to be transient and have no long-term interest in the apartment or the development. Consequently, they don't have the same concern for the regulations as would an owner-occupier.

If you're renting out your apartment, it's up to you - and not the Managing Agent - to ensure that your tenants are aware of the House Rules. If your tenants break these rules, you're the person who'll be held responsible to the Management Company, and not your tenants.

Duties and obligations of the owner

The list of duties and obligations of the Lessee - the covenants made by the owner - are fairly standard amongst apartment developments in Ireland. Apart from those mentioned below, there may also be additional rules specific to your development.

If you check your Lease you'll find most, or all, of these in there:

Pay the rent outlined in your Lease

As you're leasing your apartment from the Lessor for several hundred years, there's a rent to be paid. Notwithstanding the fact that the rent is a nominal amount – usually about €1 per year - you're legally obliged to pay it, so it must be included as a condition in your Lease. In most cases, nobody bothers to come looking for it.

Pay the Service Charges

There'll be detailed provisions in your Lease as to how the Service Charges are calculated in relation to your apartment and the time scale for payment. You must pay them according to the terms of the Lease. This rule, or a rule elsewhere in the Lease, will also provide for the imposition of interest charges if you don't pay the Service Charges in time. The Board of Directors of your Management Company is legally bound to charge interest if your Service Charges are in arrears, and you're legally obliged to pay it. Service Charges are dealt with in greater detail in chapter 6.

Keep your apartment in good repair and decorative order

This rule exists so that your apartment will be in good condition when you surrender it to the Management Company at the end of your Lease term – normally anywhere from five hundred years upwards - because, legally speaking, the Management Company owns your apartment. From that point of view, this is purely a technical point.

However, if you have a situation in your development whereby an occupier is completely neglecting the apartment - it's filthy and causing unpleasant smells and perhaps a health hazard - the Board of Directors can invoke this rule to force the owner to remedy the situation.

Dispose of your domestic waste in accordance with the House Rules

Every Board of Directors controls its refuse in its own individual way, relative to the physical nature of the development and the Local Authority regulations.

Although it usually doesn't take much effort to comply with this rule, there'll always be occupiers in every development who dump their rubbish in flimsy plastic bags anywhere and everywhere causing considerable extra work for the cleaners and a great deal of frustration for the other occupiers. This situation is sometimes aggravated by the impractical locations of the bin stores - a result of poor design by the developer's architects.

Some Boards of Directors include in the annual budget a cost for issuing one standard black refuse bag to each apartment each week. The cleaners put them into each individual mailbox on an appointed day. This can lead to a great overall improvement in the management of refuse and the maintenance of the bin stores, particularly in developments with large numbers of tenants.

A particular problem arises when new owners are in the process of moving into an apartment. This activity generates a large amount of 'non-domestic' refuse – packaging from flat-pack furniture, domestic appliances, etc., not to mention carpet cuttings, empty paint cans and other contractors' waste. The new owners and their contractors shouldn't use the bin stores to dispose of this type of material, as it's quite clearly 'non-domestic' waste. However, the practice is that most of this type of waste ends up in the bin stores and the Managing Agent has to deal with it. The additional costs end up in the annual budget - and on your Service Charge invoice. It's usually impractical to try to identify the culprits.

This can be an enormous problem in a new apartment development where dozens of new owners are moving in at the same time. It costs a considerable amount of money to have this rubbish removed and this can affect the funds remaining in the initial annual budget.

Use your car space, if any, only for a private car or motorcycle

In most apartment developments, it's not permitted to park commercial vehicles in the car spaces. Occupiers will sometimes dispute the exact definition of a 'commercial vehicle'. Is a small two seater vanette with no commercial markings on it and used only by the owner in a private capacity a commercial vehicle or a private vehicle? Some day a court may be asked to determine this issue, but in my opinion, if a vehicle is taxed as a commercial vehicle it's not unreasonable for the Board of Directors to regard it as a commercial vehicle.

The subject of car parks and car parking is also considered later in this chapter.

Not to make noise that's a nuisance to others

The typical wording of this obligation as found in many Leases is:

"*The Lessee must not play or permit to be played any musical instrument, television, radio or mechanical or other noise making instrument of any kind whatsoever or permit singing to be practised in the apartment so as to cause annoyance to others or to be audible outside the apartment between the hours of 10.00pm and 8.00am*".

The stated hours will vary between Leases in different developments.

The broad meaning of this regulation is that it's forbidden to make any noise that's audible outside your apartment between the stated hours, or to make any noise, at any time, which causes annoyance to other occupiers.

This regulation is open to interpretation and causes problems in several areas:

- It's an unfortunate fact that the standard of sound insulation in modern apartment developments is inadequate. This leads to the regular situation whereby you're able to hear almost all movements and sounds coming from the adjacent or overhead apartments, particularly at night time - regardless of how quiet your neighbours try to be. Also, that which is considered 'reasonable' noise, and that which is considered 'nuisance' noise, are very much personal to individual occupiers. This can lead to bitter disputes among neighbours - disputes which most occupiers expect the Managing Agent to be able to resolve.
- It's fairly clear that the playing of sound-making equipment (radios, stereos, TV's, musical instruments, etc.) at excessive volume is forbidden under this regulation. But what is the definition of 'excessive'? If such equipment can be heard outside the apartment during the daytime hours, and the neighbouring occupier considers it an 'annoyance', but the occupier playing the equipment considers it 'reasonable', how can the matter be determined?
- Does the wording of the regulation mean that you can't take a power shower or use your washing machine - both of which can be quite noisy - between 10pm and 8am, or at any time that might cause annoyance to your neighbours? Should they be interpreted as 'noise-making machines', or merely machines that happen to make noise when operated?
- Many people are light sleepers and will awaken or remain awake at the slightest sound. This often leads to particularly bitter disputes between neighbours where occupiers are expected to virtually creep around their apartment at night for fear of receiving a complaining knock on the wall or phone

call from a light-sleeping neighbour.

In all of these cases an element of compromise should prevail, but unfortunately, that's not always the case. The aggrieved occupier usually contacts the Managing Agent and tells him to sort it out. However, if the occupier who is accused of making the noise insists that he's doing nothing unreasonable and that he's not making excessive noise, the Managing Agent isn't in a position to take the matter any further without clear and unambiguous evidence that the rules have been breached. It's up the the aggrieved occupier to make a sufficient case to the Managing Agent.

The Managing Agent cannot act as an arbitrator in this matter and, if the dispute can't be resolved between the neighbours, the matter will have to be referred by the aggrieved occupier to the only forum that can make a legal judgement on this matter - the courts.

No universal statutory noise standards apply in Ireland and this makes the matter even more difficult to resolve.

If you feel that the noise from a neighbour's apartment is excessive and is causing you annoyance, you need to gather sufficient evidence to prove your case. Here are some suggestions:

- The chances are that annoyance is also being caused to other neighbouring occupiers, so you should contact them and make a collective complaint.
- You could make recordings of the noise as a help to demonstrate that the noise is excessive.
- You could call on some of the directors of the Management Company who live in your development to witness the noise and corroborate your complaint.
- You could bring a case against the occupier to the District Court under Section 108 of the Environmental Protection Agency Act, 1992. It's relatively simple and inexpensive to do this. Further details are available from your local District Court office. The District Court can order the offender to cease or abate the noise and the penalties for non-compliance range from a fine up to imprisonment.

If the Managing Agent is satisfied that a breach of the noise regulations has taken place - and a conviction in the District Court would be sufficient evidence - he's then in a position to take action under the terms of the Lease - see page 57.

Parties: Noisy, unruly parties are extremely disruptive in an apartment development and such parties are almost always held in apartments which have been rented to tenants.

Not only is there an excessive noise factor present, extending well into the night, but you also have the added annoyances of beer bottles and cans scattered all over the place, vomit or half eaten food on the stairwells and in the lifts, and perhaps other damage.

If you're the unfortunate neighbour of one of these parties, the first thing that's most important for you to do is to check out the identity of the apartment in question. This will probably entail having to leave your own apartment and locate the source of the party so that you're absolutely certain of the identity of the apartment. There's no point in making a complaint to the Managing Agent without being able to identify the apartment. Without information as to the identity of the apartment, there's nothing he can do.

Assuming that the apartment is readily identifiable and there's sufficient evidence that a noisy and unruly party has taken place, the Managing Agent on receipt of the complaint should immediately notify the owner in writing that a breach of the Lease has occurred. There should be an administration charge for this - see page 57. The Managing Agent should then arrange for a clean-up of any mess and the repair of any damage caused in the common areas. The additional cost of this work, including administration fees for arranging the contractors, should be charged to the owner, who is legally obliged to pay under the terms of the Lease. The owner may offer to carry out the clean-up and any repairs himself and it's up to the Managing Agent to make a decision based on reasonable grounds to accept or reject this offer.

This usually solves the problem. Most owner-landlords in these circumstances don't waste any time in issuing eviction notices to their offending tenants. If it's an owner-occupier who has thrown the party - and this is quite rare - they're unlikely to do so again, as they know the consequences if they do.

If the problem persists, further action can be taken under the terms of the Lease - see page 57.

A good Managing Agent can also alleviate the problem of parties by issuing a circular or letter to all owners and occupiers - in late November, just before the start of the Christmas celebrations - warning of the consequences of parties and the costs that might be incurred.

Alarms: Alarm activation is another noise problem which occurs frequently and can turn into a severe headache for Managing Agents and occupiers.

When an alarm activates, the alarm siren will generally sound both on the exterior and in the interior of the apartment.

Some Local Authorities have issued guidelines in relation to intruder alarms. The National Standards Authority has issued a 'standard specifications' (No. 199 of 1987) which specifies a maximum period of time for the sounding of an external alarm. At the time of writing, the period is 30 minutes. A European Standard (EN 50131-1 of 1997) specifies a shorter period of time - 15 minutes.

These Standards are voluntary and unfortunately are not legally binding.

If an alarm is sounding in your development and will not deactivate, you should first contact the Managing Agent to see if he can either:

- Make contact with the apartment owner - if he has suitable contact information on file.
- Make contact with one of the nominated keyholders - if the owner isn't contactable and he has keyholder information on file.

If neither of these possibilities are successful, there's absolutely nothing else that anybody can do about the problem until the owner or occupier returns and deactivates the alarm. There's no point in harassing the Managing Agent to 'do something', because there's nothing he, nor the Gardaí, nor the Fire Department, nor the alarm company, can legally do to deactivate the alarm.

This unfortunate and frustrating situation is a regular occurrence in apartment developments and housing estates.

In an apartment development or private 'gated' development, the problem could be alleviated if each owner furnished sufficient contact information to the Managing Agent and also nominated at least two keyholders for their apartment or house. Make sure the keyholders know the alarm codes to turn it off! See further discussion about keyholders at page 61.

Persistent alarm problems: If there's a false alarm activating on a regular basis from an apartment and causing you annoyance you can:

- Contact your Managing Agent who should insist that the owner rectify the recurring problem.
- Make application to the District Court for an order under Section 108 of the Environmental Protection Agency Act, 1992 - see above.
- Contact your Local Authority which has the power to issue a Notice to the owner under Section 107 of the Environmental Protection Agency Act, 1992.

Not to erect any external wireless, television aerial or satellite dish
The unauthorized erection of satellite dishes is becoming a regular issue in many apartment developments. This is a very difficult problem for a Managing Agent to resolve if the owner or occupier is uncooperative.

Satellite dishes can cause a development to look shabby and unattractive and it can take quite some time to persuade the offending owner or occupier to remove it. In most cases, the occupier has already spent a good deal of money in buying and erecting the dish and is therefore extremely reluctant to take it down.

It's expressly forbidden in most Leases for occupiers to erect any aerial or satellite dish in any place where it's visible to other occupiers. If the owner refuses to remove an offending satellite dish, the Managing Agent, on instruction from the Board of Directors, is entitled under the terms of the Lease to physically remove it.

It can be quite expensive to professionally remove such an item, particularly if it's located in an awkward position on the exterior of the apartment building. Any costs in removing the dish should be charged to the owner of the apartment together with any appropriate administration fees.

It's also important to remember that the erection of a satellite dish, in many circumstances, requires Planning Permission.

Not to hang clothes or bedclothes in the windows or on the balcony and not to shake any mats, carpets, sheets or duvets from any apartment window
Most owners will agree that these practices will make any apartment development look unattractive and it's for this reason that the restriction is found in most Leases. The criterion in relation to the hanging of clothes or bedclothes is that the clothes must not be visible from any part of the common areas.

Not to keep any bird or animal which, in the opinion of the Management Company, may cause annoyance or inconvenience to others
Some Leases forbid the keeping of any animals or birds in the apartment under any circumstances, but most Leases have a provision that they are permitted - provided they don't cause any annoyance to other occupiers.

What constitutes 'annoyance' or 'inconvenience' has not been clarified and is very much a matter of personal preference and opinion. Most apartments and apartment developments are not suitable environments for domestic animals - particularly dogs.

As in the case of 'excessive' noise, this is a situation where the Managing Agent must be very careful in dealing with the issue.

If there's a dispute between neighbours in relation to a domestic animal, the only forum which has the power to determine whether or not the terms of the Lease are being breached is the courts. If the disputing neighbours are stubborn on this issue, it'll have to be determined in that way and it's up to the aggrieved occupier to take the necessary action.

It's open to any person to contact the Irish Society for the Prevention of Cruelty to Animals if they believe that an animal is being kept in unsuitable conditions.

Not to exhibit any signpost or advertisement in the apartment window

This rule applies to any type of sign or advertising board of any kind. The type of sign which mainly falls for consideration under this rule is a 'For Sale' or 'To Let' sign.

There are various issues which arise with these types of signs:

Signs placed in the common areas: Whether specifically referred to in the Lease or not, it's forbidden for an owner to erect any sign on or in any location which forms part of the common area of the development - the outer walls, railings, etc.

There are two considerations here:

- Many Leases state that the Board of Directors can make regulations in relation to the common areas. In those circumstances, an owner could seek permission to place a 'For Sale' / 'To Let' sign in part of the common areas and the Board of Directors has the discretion to grant or refuse such permission. The Managing Agent doesn't have any authority to make such a decision. If you're unhappy with the decision of the Board of Directors, you could take the matter up at a General Meeting of the Management Company in an effort to persuade the Board of Directors to change its decision. However, the directors may still decide not to change their minds.
- If there's no provision in the Lease for the Board of Directors to make regulations in relation to the common areas, it could be argued that it can't grant permission for signs to be erected in the common areas as it would be acting beyond its authority.

Signs placed in your apartment window: Most Leases expressly forbid the placing of signs in apartment windows under any circumstances. The Board of Directors isn't in a position to overrule this regulation because it forms a specific term of the Lease.

Some Leases have a wording which is slightly different and which forbids signs and advertisements in an apartment window, but adds a provision that it would be lawful to exhibit a sign advertising the sale or letting of an apartment, provided the sign is first approved by the Board of Directors. This rule implies that the approval should not be unreasonably withheld. If there's such a provision in your Lease and you wish to exhibit a standard auctioneer's sign in your window, I believe that you'd be entitled to do so, provided you first obtain the approval of the Board of Directors before you erect the sign.

The Managing Agent is not in a position to grant such approval unless the Board of Directors has given him the authority to do so.

Other variations to the wording of this rule can also be found. Some Leases forbid any sign that is *"visible from the exterior of the apartment"*. Other Leases forbid signs that are *"visible from the common areas"*. If this particular wording is in your Lease and the windows of your apartment face out onto the public street, I believe that you'd be entitled to place a sign or advertisement in your window - provided that Planning Permission wasn't required - as it wouldn't be visible from the common areas.

Not to fit wooden floors

Many Leases expressly forbid the fitting of wooden floors in the apartment, stating that the floors must be covered with carpet - with the exception of the kitchen and bathroom areas where it's usually permitted to fit linoleum or some similar covering. The reasoning behind this rule is to reduce the amount of noise coming from neighbouring apartments caused by occupiers walking across wooden floors, moving furniture around, etc.

Some Leases permit the laying of wooden floors provided a suitable noise-reducing material is also fitted. They often specify the exact type and gauge of material to be used.

If you're thinking of buying a second-hand apartment which has some wooden floors in it, you should check out this provision in the Lease. If these types of floors are forbidden and you encounter a neighbour who makes a complaint about the noise coming from your apartment, the directors of the Management Company are under a legal obligation in accordance with the Lease to insist that you fit carpets on the floors.

If you refuse to do so, they can issue legal proceedings against you.

Not to let part only of your premises

The 'premises' is usually defined in the Lease as your apartment, your balcony and your car space, if any.

It's a regular practice that owner-landlords let their car space separate to their apartment and some owner-occupiers also rent out their car space if they themselves don't have a car. This principle of 'part letting' is forbidden in most Leases, but the practice appears to be fairly widespread.

If you live in your apartment and rent out one of your bedrooms to a tenant, it could be argued that you're also in breach of this rule.

Not to use the apartment for anything other than a single private residence

This rule forbids an owner or occupier from carrying on a business in their apartment. However, the custom is increasing that more and more people are working from home, so this rule might not be as straightforward as it first seems.

If a Board of Directors wishes to take issue with an owner under this rule it would need to consider:

- What is the nature of the commercial activity?
- Do members of the public visit the apartment to conduct business?
- Does the owner have employees working in the apartment?

If the owner refuses to cease the commercial operation, it may be a matter for the courts to interpret whether or not the terms of the Lease have been breached.

Balcony regulations

If your apartment has a private balcony, there'll be a section in your Lease dealing with your legal 'ownership' of it and it'll probably be dealt with in one of two ways:

- The balcony will be leased to you for the same number of years as your apartment.
- You'll be granted a licence to use the balcony for the duration of your apartment Lease. This is the more common approach in Leases.

In both cases, the fact is that you'll have exclusive use and enjoyment of your balcony. You may also find a regulation in your Lease *"not to use the balcony in a manner which would be inconsistent with the maintenance of the development as a high class development".*

What exactly does that mean?

You certainly can't hang clothes out to dry on your balcony – that'll be covered under a separate rule. You also can't leave bags of household rubbish on the balcony as, again, that'll be dealt with under another rule. But can you store other items on the balcony, like your bike or some of your children's playthings? Will that interfere with the 'high class' nature of the development? It's all a matter of personal opinion and would depend on the type of activity involved. This could be quite a headache for the Managing Agent and, if serious enough, would require recourse to the courts.

There are endless situations which involve balconies, another being where an occupier keeps potted plants on the balcony and waters them on a regular basis. This water will inevitably splash down onto the balcony, or balconies, below, possibly causing inconvenience or nuisance to those occupiers. Although it would be difficult to take action against the offending owner under the balcony rule, it might be possible to do so under the catch-all 'general nuisance' rule discussed below.

An owner could also be breaking the rules if the potted plants, or any other items, were positioned in such a way that they might fall from the balcony and injure somebody walking below. Again, the Board of Directors could not force the removal of these items under the balcony rules, but could probably do so under the 'insurance' rule discussed below.

Not to make any structural alterations to your apartment or decorate the exterior without prior permission of the Board of Directors

This obligation appears in all Leases in various forms.

This is one of the regulations which will remind you that you don't legally own your apartment – you're merely renting it for a long number of years. Even though you've spent a small fortune buying your apartment, you'll almost certainly discover that your Lease expressly forbids you to make any internal alterations to it or to paint the exterior.

If you decide to ignore the rules and proceed with structural alterations in your apartment, the Board of Directors can and should issue legal proceedings against you to stop you.

In 1999, the owner of an apartment in South Dublin decided to install a wooden floor in his apartment and also erect a studded partition in his living room, both of which were in contravention of the terms of his Lease. Legal proceedings were instituted against him by the Board of Directors. The owner lost his case in the Circuit Court and was ordered to reinstate the apartment into its original condition. Not only was that an expensive enough operation, but the owner was also ordered by the Court to pay £7,500 in damages to the Management Company and to pay all legal costs.

If you wish to make some structural alterations to the interior of your apartment and the directors of the Management Company refuse to permit it and you feel that they've acted unreasonably, you should contact your legal advisers. The Board of Directors must act and make decisions primarily in the best interests of the Management Company. However, they must also act and use their discretion in a reasonable manner.

In many Leases, the Board of Directors is given no authority to grant such permission . If that's the case in your Lease, even if there are no objections to the alterations, such alterations can never go ahead.

This regulation also applies to balconies where an owner proposes to enclose his balcony with glass or windows. This would be considered a 'structural alteration'. Depending on the provisions of the Lease, he might be able to seek permission from the Board of Directors. It's unlikely that permission could ever be granted if the owner only has a licence to use the balcony. There might also be planning issues to be considered and these would be the responsibility of the owner to resolve.

Excessive weight, dangerous materials and additional insurance risk rules

There are various rules contained in most Leases to the effect that:

- You can't bring into your apartment or balcony anything which might cause excess weight or strain on the structure.
- You can't keep petrol or other dangerous or explosive materials anywhere in your apartment or balcony.
- You can't do anything, or permit anything to be done, which may render void the insurances or result in an increase in the insurance premium.

These rules are contained in the Lease for the common protection of all owners.

Comply with and observe all rules and regulations made by the Board of Directors in relation to the common areas

Any rules made by the Board of Directors should be made in the interests of the company and for the benefit of all owners, but that doesn't mean that all owners will agree with them.

This may be the case in relation to car parking regulations in particular. Many Leases have a specific provision giving power to the Board of Directors to make regulations in relation to the car parking area, such as the marking of car spaces, the hiring of clamping companies, etc. The issues surrounding car parking are dealt with in greater detail further on in this chapter.

There may also be situations where the Board of Directors decides to relocate the bike racks or the bin store, or switch off certain floodlights which it deems to be expensive or unnecessary. The directors have the power to take this action under this regulation without obtaining the permission of the owners.

As an owner, you can seek to have these decisions changed or reversed either at the Annual General Meeting, or by calling an Extraordinary General Meeting. The directors at such a meeting are not obliged to follow any resolutions passed in this regard by the owners - because it's the Board of Directors that is empowered to manage the development, not the owners. If the directors feel that such resolutions are contrary to the proper management of the development, they can refuse to implement them.

However, in certain circumstances, the owners can reverse or influence some decisions of the Board of Directors by amending the Articles of Association of the company and inserting specific provisions to deal with the issue. See page 122.

Permit the Management Company or its agents to enter your apartment in order to fulfil its obligations

There are occasions when the Board of Directors may wish to gain access to, or send contractors into, your apartment. You must allow them access.

Perhaps there may be a problem in one of the neighbouring apartments - probably an electrical or plumbing problem - and it may be necessary to examine your apartment in an effort to find out where the problem is originating. In this case, the Board of Directors has the legal right to do whatever is necessary - take down panelling or ceilings to expose pipework, etc. - in order to try to get to the source of the problem. You must give them access to whatever areas they wish to investigate, and not impede them at their work.

Any damage caused to the interior of your apartment by such work must be repaired and made good at no cost to yourself. If, however, it transpires that the source of the problem comes from your own apartment, you yourself may have to bear the costs.

Some apartment block insurance policies cover the cost, or some of the cost, of locating water leaks. You should check the apartment block insurance policy if you've a problem in this area.

If an owner refuses to allow the Board of Directors access to his apartment, or if the owner or occupier can't be contacted, it's my opinion that the Board of Directors, in the common interest of all owners, may force entry in order to sort out a serious problem. This action should only be taken in the event of an emergency.

If such a situation is likely to occur, it would be highly advisable for all parties to seek legal advice before taking any action, but this may not be possible in the case of an emergency.

Restrain from doing anything which may cause nuisance to the Management Company or any of the owners or occupiers

This is the 'catch-all' rule and is to be found in every apartment Lease. If an owner or occupier is doing something which is causing a nuisance to other owners but the activity in question is not covered under any other specific regulation in the Lease, the Board of Directors can insist that the occupier cease the particular activity under this rule.

Fully and effectively indemnify the Management Company

There's a provision in many Leases - though not in every Lease - to the effect that the owner must fully indemnify the Management Company against any breach of the Lease, and must also indemnify the Management Company against any costs, outlay, or expenses incurred as a result of any such breach. This is a very important regulation and can be a very useful tool in dealing with owners or occupiers who are in breach of the terms of the Lease.

This provision allows the Board of Directors to levy a reasonable financial charge on any owner who is in breach of the rules and where there has been an expense incurred in resolving the issue. In my opinion, this expense should also include the time spent by the Board of Directors and/or Managing Agent in dealing with the matter.

The most significant area where this is most likely to arise is the non-payment of Service Charges. Almost every development has problems with the non-payment of Service Charges by some owners. In my opinion, every owner who doesn't pay their Service Charge in accordance with the terms of the Lease should incur administration charges to cover the cost of pursuing and collecting the Service Charge arrears. These fees may include VAT if the Managing Agent is charging the fee to the owner - see page 91.

Similarly, if the occupiers of an apartment are in breach of the rules

- noise, leaving refuse bags on balconies, unauthorised satellite dishes, etc. - the Managing Agent will have to write to the individuals, notify them of the breach and demand that it be rectified. He'll also have to monitor the situation until it has been rectified.

Under this provision of the Lease, I believe that the Board of Directors is fully entitled to charge a reasonable sum to the apartment owner to cover the expense of dealing with the matter. If the offending party is a tenant, it's the owner-landlord who is liable to the Management Company for any breaches of the rules by his tenants and the owner-landlord should be charged for the time and effort spent in dealing with the matter. It's up to the owner-landlord as to how he handles the matter with his tenant in such a case.

If, however, your lease doesn't contain the specific 'fully and effectively indemnify' clause, I believe that it's an implied term of the Lease that every owner is liable for any costs incurred by the Management Company in dealing with any breach of the regulations. Therefore, the Board of Directors or Managing Agent would still be entitled to charge a reasonable amount to an offending owner for their time and effort in dealing with any breach of the Lease, even if there's no specific mention of such a charge in the Lease itself.

Remedies for breaches of the rules

In every Lease, the Management Company, through the Board of Directors, undertakes to do everything in its power to ensure that all owners comply with the terms of the Lease. Prior to the handing over of the development, it's the developer who gives this guarantee.

If an owner is in breach of the terms of the Lease, the Board of Directors is under a legal obligation to all other owners to rectify the situation. A warning letter from the Managing Agent will normally resolve most problems.

However, if the owner or occupier persists in the breach of the Lease, the Board of Directors must institute legal proceedings against him and the matter should be placed in the hands of the Management Company's solicitor. Depending on the nature of the breach and the wording of the Lease, there'll be various options open to the solicitor.

The most specific option open to the Board of Directors, and contained in every Lease, is to institute proceedings in the Circuit Court against the offending owner for forfeiture of his Lease. This would mean that the Management Company would get possession of the apartment. It's unlikely that any court is going to grant forfeiture of the Lease, but it can award damages, which, when coupled with the legal expenses, will be very costly to the offending owner.

There's also an argument to be made that the owner's lending institution should be informed of any impending legal proceedings for forfeiture, as they're in danger of losing their asset.

I don't think any lending institution would tolerate this situation. The owner could find himself under considerable pressure to resolve the problem.

It's very rare for an owner to allow a case to go to court in circumstances where he's clearly in breach of the Lease.

Refusal to take action

If the Managing Agent refuses or fails to deal with an obvious breach of the Lease by an owner, you have the following possible options available to you:

- Request that the Board of Directors - or the developer if the development hasn't yet been handed over - dismiss the Managing Agent and appoint another one - see page 36.
- Seek legal advice from your solicitor with a view to instituting legal proceedings against the Board of Directors and/or the offending owner for possible breach of contract.
- Seek to change the Board of Directors at a General Meeting of the Company.
- Seek to amend the Articles of Association of the company to permit the owners to dismiss the Managing Agent and appoint a new one - see page 122.

Troublesome neighbours and how to deal with them

A large amount of the time and effort spent by Managing Agents in managing an apartment development has little to do with *property* management. It has more to do with the management and control of *people*.

There are thousands of unreasonable people living all around us - the type of people who stroll through life without caring one iota about their fellow citizens and who carry on exactly as they wish, without the slightest regard for the inconvenience, nuisance and annoyance which they're causing to others by their actions. These are the people who believe that rules exist for everybody else but not for them. As long as they can do exactly what they want, they don't care how much inconvenience or annoyance they cause to other people.

These individuals are out there - on the roads, in the pubs, in your workplace. And, unfortunately - and inevitably - in your apartment development.

Tenants

In my experience, tenants in apartments don't have the same regard for the development as would an owner-occupier; nor do they have as much regard for the considerations of their neighbours.

That might sound like quite a generalisation, and I'm aware that there are tenants who don't fall into this category. However, I don't exaggerate when I say that, of all of the breaches of House Rules which I dealt with as a Managing Agent - quite a considerable number - I reckon that about 90% involved the activities of tenants in rented apartments.

What should you do if your enjoyment of life in your apartment is being disrupted by inconsiderate and anti-social tenants?

1st Move: You could always consider approaching the offending occupier directly. The occupier may be unaware of the inconvenience he's causing or may not be aware that he's breaking one of the House Rules. If the tenant is reasonable, this can sometimes be the speediest and most convenient way to solve the problem.

2nd Move: If you choose not to make the first move yourself or you've done so to no avail, you should contact your Managing Agent. He should contact the occupiers and demand that they cease the stated misbehaviour - provided that it's an obvious breach of the House Rules and not one over which there's a difference of opinion.

The owner-landlord should also be contacted by the Managing Agent and informed of the problem, as he's responsible for the actions of his tenants. He should be advised to speak to his tenants to ensure that there are no further breaches of the House Rules.

3rd Move: If the owner and occupier ignore the issue and the breach of the House Rules persists, the Managing Agent should advise the Board of Directors to contact the Management Company's solicitor and institute legal proceedings against the owner for:

- Forfeiture of the Lease.
- Damages.
- Costs.

The Board of Directors is under a legal obligation to take this action. It's one of the promises it made to you when the Management

Company directors signed your Lease.

Before issuing the Circuit Court summons, the solicitor will send a formal notice to the owner and his lending institution to indicate that legal proceedings for forfeiture would be taken if the breach of the House Rules continued. If, after about twenty-eight days, the situation hasn't been resolved, the solicitor should start the legal proceedings. All costs involved should be levied against the owner as per the terms of the Lease - see page 55.

It's unlikely that the owner, and in particular the lending institution, will ignore the notice from the Management Company's solicitor and if they do, the case should proceed to court - see page 53.

If you're having a problem with an anti-social neighbour, you must be prepared for the fact that a solution to the problem is unlikely to occur overnight. If the tenants prove to be awkward individuals and the landlord has to take them to court in order to evict them, there's nothing anyone can do until the legal system takes its course.

There can also be a further problem if the Managing Agent experiences difficulty contacting the owner-landlord because of a lack of adequate information - see below.

Owner-occupiers

If the offending neighbour is an owner-occupier, the same procedures as above will apply with the exception that there'll be no tenants to contact – just the owner himself. It'll also be easier for the Managing Agent to make contact with the owner, as, in this case, he's the occupier of the apartment.

Contact information

Owners

One of the greatest problems that a Managing Agent can have is that he hasn't any contact details for an owner - such as phone number or email address - when he needs to contact him in a hurry.

There's no legal obligation on any owner to furnish this information to the Managing Agent, but it's in every owner's interest to do so in order to be quickly contactable should a problem arise.

The best time to get this information in a new development is when the apartment is sold for the first time. However, very often the developer's solicitor isn't given this information and the address for the owner is recorded as being the apartment which he has just purchased, even though the owner might be an investor and, therefore, won't be living there.

Some Managing Agents send out forms on an annual basis - usually with the Service Charge invoice - requesting that certain contact details be provided by each owner, or an update on the information already provided. Unfortunately, the majority of owners tend not to return these forms.

A Managing Agent may need to contact an owner for a variety of reasons, ranging from such simple situations as confirming the correct address for communications, to problems with tenants, or emergencies such as burglaries, water leaks, etc.

In the event of being unable to contact an owner, the Managing Agent must then try to make contact with the occupier of the apartment who is usually a tenant. If this is successful, the tenant can provide details of their landlord or the letting agency. Sometimes tenants refuse to give this information to the Managing Agent - they're not legally obliged to do so.

If that doesn't work, then it's necessary to contact the solicitor who represented the owner in the purchase of the apartment. This information is not usually provided to the Managing Agent at the time of purchase, so if that's the case, it'll be necessary to contact the developer's solicitor for him to look up his files and provide the information about the purchaser's solicitor.

When the owner's solicitor is contacted, he might not furnish any contact details about his client until he has obtained the permission from his client to do so.

At this stage, all that the Managing Agent can hope for is that the solicitor is successful in contacting the owner and the owner makes contact directly, or gives permission for the solicitor to provide the relevant contact information.

It can take many days to contact an owner in this fashion and it's totally impractical in the case of emergencies or the behaviour of anti-social tenants. It can also be enormously time-consuming for the Managing Agent.

Owners should be encouraged by the Managing Agent to supply all relevant contact information, and update it on an annual basis.

There's always the possibility that the owner in question is an owner-occupier and is merely away from his home for a period of time. If this is the case, and there's an urgency to gain access to the apartment, it's vital that the Managing Agent is able to contact other keyholders.

Keyholders

The day-to-day management of an apartment development would be less troublesome if owners appointed at least two keyholders - who have access to the apartment and any alarm codes - and provided contact details for these keyholders to the Managing Agent.

It's a relatively simple thing to do and would give peace-of-mind to both the owner and the Managing Agent.

Unfortunately, very few owners bother to do this.

Tenants

Although it would be convenient for a Managing Agent to have contact details for tenants, it isn't very practical for a number of reasons:

- If the owner-landlord is renting out the apartment through a letting agency there's a strong likelihood that he himself doesn't have any contact details for his tenants.
- The task becomes unworkable if there's a large number of tenanted apartments in the development . Firstly, it can be difficult to obtain the information from either the owner-landlord or his letting agent. Secondly, the information will require updating every six/twelve months as the tenants change.

A remedy

The best method of resolving the problem of providing contact information is to incorporate it as one of the terms of the Lease before the apartments are sold, or amend the Articles of Association of the Company, to make it a legal obligation for the owner to:

- Provide to the Managing Agent full details in relation to his mailing address and contact phone numbers, emails, etc.
- Ensure that the Managing Agent is updated with contact information in relation to two other persons - keyholders - who have full access to the apartment and the alarm codes.

Security

Security has become a major issue in apartment developments in Ireland. Owners should keep in mind the following:

- There's no obligation on a developer to design and build a development so that it's secure to the satisfaction of the owners.

- In the first instance, it's the responsibility of each occupier to ensure that their own apartment and car, if any, are as secure as possible.
- There's a significant cost factor in any decision to improve security in an apartment development. The provision of CCTV cameras and recording equipment, electronic swipe-card systems or security personnel can be very expensive. These facilities are too costly for many apartment developments to consider with the exception of the very large ones.

If you feel that the security situation in your apartment development is inadequate, you should contact the Board of Directors and request them to upgrade the security facilities. The directors are not legally obliged to do so if they don't consider it necessary or if they consider that it would be too expensive.

An upgrading of security at your apartment development will inevitably lead to higher Service Charges. This is an issue which could be discussed at an informal pre-budget meeting with the owners to see if it's possible to arrive at agreement on the matter.

The Managing Agent has very limited authority when it comes to security. Apart from the obvious repairs when a break-in or vandalism occurs, the Managing Agent has no legal power to spend Management Company's funds on security unless it has been provided for in the annual budget or he has specific instructions from the Board of Directors on the matter.

The time to address the question of funds for additional security facilities is when the annual budget is being decided. Additional expenditure can then be included in the budget and passed on to the owners through the Service Charges.

The Board of Directors is empowered under the Lease to introduce an interim supplementary mid-term budget if it feels that it's necessary for the proper management of the development. This would include introducing new security facilities.

Cleaning and landscaping

The Board of Directors is legally responsible, under the terms of the Lease, to ensure that the common areas of the development are maintained to a high standard. Adequate provision must be made in the annual budget for cleaning and landscaping services and equipment.

The cleaning and landscaping policy must be affordable and relative to the size of the development and the standards expected. A development of high-class and expensive apartments in an upmarket area might be expected to spend more on the cleaning and landscaping services than a development of budget apartments situated in a less exclusive area.

Satisfying all the owners - whose opinions on what is an 'acceptable level' of cleanliness and maintenance will differ greatly - is a very difficult task.

In most apartment developments, it's not economically viable to have cleaners on site every day to clean the common areas. Most budgets simply wouldn't support it. Therefore, the Board of Directors must make a decision regarding the frequency of the cleaning and landscaping services. The major consideration in this matter will always be affordability or, more particularly, the amount of money the owners are prepared to pay for these services through their Service Charges.

In my opinion, it would be good property management practice for the Managing Agent to circulate all occupiers with the schedule for the cleaning and landscaping of the development. In that way, if the occupiers see some litter scattered around the development, they'll know on what days to expect the cleaners or landscapers to be on site to remove it. They can, of course, always remove it themselves.

Notwithstanding the above, the Managing Agent should be in a position to hire cleaners outside of the agreed cleaning schedule when specific acts of defilement have taken place - in particular, vomiting in the common areas, or worse. There should be provision made in the annual budget for this type of unscheduled expense. This is usually provided for in the 'miscellaneous repairs and renewals' section of the budget.

Graffiti

Graffiti can be a recurring problem in urban apartment developments and is an issue which causes annoyance and frustration to owners and occupiers.

The removal of graffiti is an expensive exercise and one which can cause damage to plasterwork, paintwork and brickwork. You should not expect the Managing Agent to immediately arrange for the removal of graffiti as soon as it appears, because the chances are that it will reappear again the next day.

It's reasonable to arrange for the removal of graffiti on a scheduled basis - maybe every four to six months. The Managing Agent and the Board of Directors should consult on this matter. Ultimately, it's the Board of Directors decision. Provision should be made in the budget for this type of work and perhaps for other specific cleaning tasks such as the removal of chewing-gum from pavements and walkways within the development.

Poor water supply

If you believe that the water pressure to your apartment is below an acceptable level, you should contact the Managing Agent and ask him to look into the matter.

The first thing to establish is that the correct pressure is coming from the Local Authority water main into your development. Local Authorities will carry out a pressure and flow test. There's usually a fee charged for this but the fee is refundable if it transpires that there's a problem with the Local Authority water main.

If it transpires that the flow from the public main is adequate, the Managing Agent will have to address the issue of a possible internal water problem within your development. The Managing Agent shouldn't commence any expensive investigations without instructions from the Board of Directors.

Local Authorities admit that the public water pressure can vary considerably throughout the day, the pressure being lowest at peak periods - breakfast, lunch and tea-time.

If the Board of Directors doesn't consider that there's a specific problem in your development, you'll have to arrange for a plumber to check out your own apartment. It might also be a useful exercise to check with your neighbours to see if they're experiencing any problems. If they are, you have a better chance of persuading the Board of Directors to get the Managing Agent to investigate the matter.

Car parking

The provision and management of car parking spaces is dealt with in various different ways in apartment Leases.

Unallocated spaces
In some developments, you have a situation where there's a car parking area but no spaces are allocated to individual apartments and the system operates on a 'first come, first served' basis. This

can be very inconvenient when there aren't enough spaces for all of the occupiers' cars in the development.

Depending on the wording of the Lease, the Board of Directors may be in a position to make some regulations in relation to the car park such as visitor parking, access to the car park, marking out the spaces, etc. It would be highly advisable for the Board of Directors to hold an informal owners' meeting, or an Extraordinary General Meeting, to arrive at agreement among the owners on the issue. However, it's not within its power to allocate specific spaces to owners if such provision is not contained in the Lease.

Allocated spaces

In many Leases, a specific car space is allocated to you when you buy your apartment. You often have to pay an additional sum in the purchase price for this space.

In this situation, the car space becomes part of your 'premises'. It's an extension of your apartment.

The problem arises, of course, when someone else parks in your space. This is a common and very frustrating occurrence.

You'll probably find, on investigation, that these cars belong to:
- Visitors to the development who shouldn't be able to gain access to the car park at all, but somehow manage to do so.
- Occupiers who don't have a car space.
- Occupiers who live in an apartment where there are two car owners but only one space allocated.
- Occupiers who have a car space but their own space has been usurped by another car.

So what can you do in this situation?

There isn't a lot you can do at the particular moment when you find that your space is being used by someone else. You can put a note on the windscreen of the offending car or phone the clamping company if one is engaged by the Board of Directors. But still, that doesn't get you into your space. So you either have to park somewhere outside on the public street, or park in someone else's space. The decision will be yours.

You should take the registration number of the offending car and pass it on to the Managing Agent so that he can see if any pattern emerges. If the same car keeps turning up in other occupiers' spaces on a regular basis it's much easier to deal with the situation.

Most Boards of Directors now engage private clamping companies to clamp cars which are parked in unauthorised spaces and this appears to alleviate the problem.

Commercial vehicles

Most Leases expressly forbid the parking of any vehicle other than a private car or motor bike in the car parking area.

However, it's not unusual for occupiers to park vans or even trucks in the car park.

If a complaint is made by an owner that commercial vehicles are being parked in the car park, the Managing Agent should write a note pointing out the breach of the rules and fix it to the windscreen of the vehicle. If it's possible to identify the owner of the car space, the Managing Agent can write to him directly on the issue.

It may take some time to identify the occupiers involved in a case where the commercial vehicle is parked in the visitors' spaces or in unallocated spaces. If the Managing Agent attaches a note to the windscreen of the vehicle and it's ignored, it may be necessary for him to employ somebody to sit in the car park and wait until the offending vehicle is parked and then follow the driver to the relevant apartment. Under those circumstances, it may take some time and expense to sort out. However, it should be possible to recover the expenses from the offending owner provided that such expenses were reasonably incurred.

If an owner, when approached, insists that the vehicle is not used for commercial purposes and therefore shouldn't be regarded as a 'commercial vehicle', he should be asked to produce the Vehicle Registration Certificate. It's my opinion that if it's registered and taxed as a commercial vehicle, then it can be considered as one and the Board of Directors can take appropriate action.

Access to car park

Many of the car parking problems could be eliminated if access to the car park could be confined to those who have parking permits.

However, in many developments, the bike shed and bin stores are located in the car park and this means that all occupiers must have access to it.

Marking spaces

In some cases, the individual parking spaces have not been marked out by the developer and this can lead to erratic parking causing complete wastes of valuable space. In this situation, the Board of Directors should engage contractors to mark out the spaces. This is an expensive operation which might need the insertion of specific provisions in the annual budget to cater for it.

The marking of the spaces is a decision for the Board of Directors. The Managing Agent has no legal authority to do this, so there's no point in pestering him to mark out the spaces if the Board of Directors won't make the decision or isn't prepared to allocate funds to pay for it.

In some blocks, the Board of Directors or Managing Agent might suggest the marking of each space with the individual apartment number as an encouragement to stop unauthorised parking in the space. In some developments, the spaces are already marked out in this manner by the developer.

There's no evidence to suggest that this will discourage others from parking in your space. It could also be argued that there's a security risk attached. If your car space is empty, then everybody who's in the car park at that time knows that there's probably nobody at home in your apartment.

Although it's a matter over which the Board of Directors would have authority, I suggest that an informal meeting of all owners be held to obtain their consent before marking out car spaces with apartment numbers.

Space too small

In new developments, Managing Agents frequently receive complaints from occupiers that:

- Their car space is too small.
- It's location is different from the original plans.
- There's some obstruction - access doors, support columns, etc. - in a position whereby it's almost impossible to park in the space.

These are all matters concerning the Legal Title and occupancy of your premises. It's not a matter in which the Managing Agent has any role at all.

If you're experiencing such a problem, you should contact the auctioneer who sold you the apartment and he should be able to sort it out with the developer. If that approach isn't successful, you'll need to contact your solicitor.

Renting out your car space

It's usually forbidden in the Lease to rent out your car space to another person, even to another apartment owner or occupier in your development. Your car park space, along with your apartment and balcony, form what's legally described in your Lease as the 'premises'. Most Leases state quite clearly that it's forbidden to rent out part only of your premises.

Nevertheless, the practice is widespread throughout city centre apartment developments. If a complaint is made to the Board of Directors about this practice, it's legally bound under the Lease to take action against the offending owner.

Stolen vehicles

Apartment car parks, particularly underground car parks, are fairly private and sheltered places and they're frequently used by thieves to store and hide stolen cars until such time as they need them for use in robberies.

If you observe any suspicious activity or suspicious vehicles in your car park, you should report the matter to the Managing Agent or the Gardaí immediately.

Bicycles

In most apartment developments, there's an area set aside for the parking or storing of bikes. It's usually in the form of a bike shed. Unfortunately, not all occupiers or their visitors will go to the trouble of using the bike shed and many of them will lock their bikes to the nearest railings, or, worse still, bring them into the hallways of the apartment buildings. This is forbidden under the terms of most Leases, which usually state that bikes must not be stored or kept in any part of the common areas other than in the bike shed.

In order to try to relieve this problem, the Managing Agent should display suitable signs prohibiting the parking of bikes in unauthorized areas. If this doesn't work, further action should be considered.

As a Managing Agent, I experienced serious problems with bikes in certain developments and owners regularly complained to me about the situation. I suggested to various Boards of Directors that 'offending' bikes should be removed with a bolt-cutter, safely stored somewhere, and only returned to the owners when a suitable fee was paid.

The action of removing the bikes in this way sorted out the problem fairly quickly, although it gave rise to some extremely abusive and threatening phone calls!

If any Board of Directors decides to take this action, it's important that the Managing Agent sends circulars to all owners and occupiers and also erects signs to inform all owners and visitors about the 'bike removal policy'. It's also the responsibility of the Board of Directors to ensure that the area allotted for bikes is suitable and as secure and safe as is reasonably possible.

Lift maintenance contracts

The maintenance of lifts, and making provision in the Sinking Fund for their replacement, are two expensive items in most annual budgets.

Some lift maintenance companies provide different levels of service with their annual contracts, from the very basic statutory maintenance contract up to a comprehensive twenty-four hour call-out service. If you're concerned about this matter, you should contact your Managing Agent and request details of the lift contract. It's the Board of Director's responsibility to decide on the level of lift maintenance contract. The directors don't have to opt for the most comprehensive contract, but it's their legal responsibility under the terms of the Lease to ensure that the lift is maintained in good working condition.

The Board of Directors must arrange a suitable engineering insurance policy for the lifts to cover statutory annual inspections - it's a criminal office not to have this insurance - see page 137.

Twenty-four hour emergency contacts

The Managing Agent should have in place an arrangement whereby a suitable individual or company can be contacted by an occupier on a twenty-four hour basis in the event of an emergency, and that the individual or company can appoint a contractor to attend at the development at short notice and at unsocial hours if necessary.

The main emergencies which are likely to arise are water leaks and damaged or broken car park gates or entrance doors. Most other so-called 'emergencies' are not immediate and can be dealt with during normal working hours.

There are two ways to make provision for twenty-four hour emergency contacts.

Firstly, the Managing Agent can appoint a person to take all emergency calls and the phone number is circulated to all occupiers. This person should have a list of suitable contractors who are available on a twenty-four hour call-out basis. If there's no Managing Agent engaged, it might be quite difficult to find a person from among the owners or directors to take on this responsibility.

The provision of this type of service is difficult because most of the

'emergency' calls which will be received at unsocial hours are either not the responsibility of the Board of Directors or Managing Agent or not genuine emergencies at all. Typical examples include:
- "I've lost my keys and can't get into the apartment".
- "There's noise coming from the apartment next door and I can't sleep".
- "There's somebody acting suspiciously in the courtyard".
- "I came into my apartment and switched on the light and the light didn't come on".

The individual employed to take the emergency calls needs to have great tolerance and patience!

The second way to deal with this issue is to display notices throughout the development with various contractors' phone numbers for occupiers to contact in the event of specified emergencies. This information could be included on the House Rules notices and a suggested format can be found in Appendix F.

Emergency call-out charges during anti-social hours are very expensive and it's important that the Managing Agent monitors the situation.

If an emergency call-out is made and it transpires that the problem was caused in an individual apartment and therefore was the responsibility of the owner, it's the owner of the apartment who must cover the costs involved.

Damp apartments

Managing Agents are sometimes contacted by owners who tell them that some of the walls of the apartment are covered in damp mould and, therefore, there must be a water leak somewhere.

I've been involved in a number of these situations and on visiting the apartments in question, I would invariably notice that the occupiers of the apartment had blocked up the exterior air vents, the windows had been sealed shut and the curtains closed even during daytime. These tenants will regularly be taking showers or baths, cooking meals and probably drying damp clothes on the radiators. In this type of environment, there'll be condensation on the walls almost permanently, leading very quickly to the appearance of damp mould.

There were never any water leaks in any of the apartments which I visited.

This problem has become so widespread that Homebond has published an information booklet on the subject of condensation and dampness in apartments, and it's available free of charge - see Appendix H for contact details.

Structural problems

If you believe that there are structural problems with your apartment or in some of the common areas of the building such as the roof, stairwells, etc., you should contact the Managing Agent to see if any other owners have made similar complaints, or if the developer or Board of Directors is aware of the situation. The Managing Agent won't have any authority or control over the matter and will have to seek instructions. If it's a new development and you consider it necessary you should contact your solicitor.

General common area maintenance

Various problems can arise in the common areas and it's the Board of Director's responsibility to resolve these issues through the Managing Agent.

Matters such as the repair of access doors and railings, automatic car park gates, lifts and lighting must be addressed immediately and dealt with as a priority, particularly where matters of Health & Safety and security are involved. Under normal circumstances, the Managing Agent should deal with these repairs without having to consult with the Board of Directors for every occurrence.

If significant expenditure is required to resolve a particular problem, the Board of Directors must make the decision and then instruct the Managing Agent to deal with the matter. If, due to the Management Company's financial position or the amount of the expenditure required, a supplementary budget is necessary, the Board of Directors must make the appropriate decisions in that regard.

Private 'gated' developments

Living in a private 'gated' development is quite different from living in an apartment. All of the maintenance, decoration and repair issues concerning the interior and exterior of your own house must be arranged, paid for and managed by you.

Most of the duties and responsibilities of owners outlined in this chapter will not apply to house owners in a private 'gated' development and if there are certain duties and responsibilities for house

owners, these will be set out in your title documents. The most important of these duties will be to:
- Pay the annual Service Charge to the Management Company for the management of the common areas, public lighting, public liability insurance, refuse collection, etc.
- Dispose of your domestic refuse in accordance with the rules.
- Obey any parking regulations.

Summary

◂ You're legally obliged to adhere to a list of rules and regulations in your development.
◂ These are set out clearly in your Lease.
◂ It's the responsibility of an owner-landlord to ensure that his tenants adhere to the House Rules and he'll be held liable for their behaviour if they don't.
◂ The Management Company, through the Board of Directors, is legally bound to ensure that the duties and obligations as set out in the Lease are adhered to by all owners and occupiers.
◂ If the Managing Agent fails to deal with occupiers who breach the Lease, an aggrieved owner can ask the Board of Directors to replace him but the Board of Directors is not obliged to do so. An aggrieved owner can try to have the Articles of Association amended to give owners greater say in the appointment and dismissal of the Managing Agent.
◂ If the Board of Directors fails to deal with occupiers who break the House Rules, an aggrieved owner can take action to institute legal proceedings against the directors or seek to replace them at a General Meeting of the Management Company.
◂ Every owner should furnish comprehensive contact details to the Managing Agent, together with contact details for at least two keyholders.

Chapter 6

Financial Matters

The financial structure of an apartment development is similar to that of a small trading company.

The Management Company, through its Board of Directors, controls and manages 'the business' of the company, which is to manage the development. The Board of Directors must also manage the legal and financial affairs of the Management Company itself.

There should be a bank account in the name of the Management Company, through which all cheque payments are made. There should also be at least one deposit or similar account for the Sinking Fund, also in the name of the Management Company.

There can be numerous current or deposit accounts depending on the needs of the development.

Budgets

Before the end of the financial year, an annual budget is prepared which estimates the amount of money required to run the development, and the Management Company itself, for the subsequent year. The budget might also include a section for any significant forthcoming capital expenditure - eg. the installation of additional security equipment, etc. Most important of all, the budget must make provision for a reasonable contribution towards the Sinking Fund.

This budget is prepared by the Board of Directors in conjunction with the Managing Agent. It must always be formally approved by the Board of Directors.

You're obliged to pay a sum of money every year to cover your portion of the anticipated expenses as set out in the annual budget. This contribution is called a Service Charge. The proportion to be paid is outlined in your Lease. It'll be calculated based on the size of your apartment or perhaps the number of bedrooms or perhaps some other criteria.

The annual budget should be presented to you in a transparent and detailed manner, and the various costings should be broken down and itemised under each budget heading on your Service Charge invoice, or elsewhere.

Many owners can't understand why their Service Charge is so high and why it seems to increase significantly every year. They think that the Service Charge only covers the cost of occasional cutting of grass or clipping of hedges, the cleaning of the corridors, the block insurance and a few other bits and pieces. These owners become very frustrated and are convinced that they're being 'ripped off' by either the Managing Agent, the Board of Directors, or both.

The main reason why owners feel this way is because they haven't been given enough detailed information in relation to the annual budget, and, therefore, aren't fully aware of the cost of managing their development. If you're in this situation, you should insist that a proper and detailed breakdown under each cost heading is given to you by the Managing Agent.

If a detailed annual budget is presented to you with your Service Charge invoice, you should carefully examine it. If you do this, you're likely to see that there's a great deal more involved in running your apartment development than might appear on the surface. It won't bring the costs down, but it might make you feel a little less suspicious.

Having said that, I also realise that there's probably an element of improper expenditure or inefficiency in some apartment developments, and this is why it's not unreasonable for owners to demand to see detailed breakdowns of the various costings.

Who decides the budget?

The Managing Agent usually prepares a draft annual budget in consultation with the Board of Directors. It's the function and legal responsibility of the Board of Directors to formally approve the annual budget and levy the Service Charges accordingly.

If the development hasn't been handed over by the developer, it's the Managing Agent who usually prepares the budget, with, or without, an input from the developer. The Managing Agent should consult with the ad-hoc owners' committee if one is in place. The budget must ultimately have the official approval of the developer under the terms of the Lease.

Some Boards of Directors hold an informal owners' meeting to discuss the budget. In my opinion, this is good practice as it gives everybody a chance to air their views on the matter. The directors, however, make the final decisions.

Once the annual budget has been decided and the Service Charge invoices have been sent out, it's the legal duty of every owner to pay the relevant Service Charge, whether or not they agree with the budget.

Initial budget in a new development

The accuracy and preparation of the first year's budget in a new development is perhaps one of the most controversial issues surrounding apartment living in Ireland today.

When a developer builds an apartment block, he must decide on the level and apportionment of Service Charges on each apartment before they go on sale, as you must pay the first year's Service Charge at the same time as you buy your apartment. At this stage, most developers have just one priority on their minds – to keep the Service Charge as low as possible in order to make the apartments as attractive as possible to potential buyers.

It's easy to strike quite a low budget in the first year of a new apartment development, or when the development hasn't yet been completed, because:

- Many of the electrical and mechanical installations - lifts, water pumps, fire alarms, etc. - will either not be commissioned or will still be under warranty and, therefore, fewer annual service contracts will be in place.
- Security matters are more than likely looked after by the developer as he has an interest in securing the site and protecting his equipment.
- There'll probably be little or no landscaping expenses because the landscaping won't be completed until the building work has been finished.
- Provision for the Sinking Fund in the budget will either be non-existent or unrealistically small.

Under these circumstances, the initial budget can be totally misleading and won't reflect the true cost of managing the development from Year 2 onwards. In some cases, the Managing Agent is instructed by the developer to make the first annual budget as low as possible. In many instances the developer will actually tell the Managing Agent the amounts of the Service Charge he intends to apply to each apartment in the development, and the Managing Agent must juggle the figures to make the first budget reflect this.

This is all very well in Year 1. You've just bought an apartment, you're moving in, the Service Charge is low, and you're happy.

But in Year 2 the inevitable occurs. The annual service contracts for the electrical and mechanical equipment, the landscaping costs, the security contracts, the Sinking Fund, etc. all become a reality. The budget dramatically increases and so does your Service Charge. You're angry and frustrated, and rightly so.

Unfortunately, there's nothing you can do at this stage but grind your teeth and bear with it. A refusal to pay the Service Charge, 'as a matter of principle', is both self-defeating and contrary to the terms of your Lease - see page 87.

So who's to blame for this situation?

The developer, without doubt, is being less than genuine with the buyers. He's aware that the Service Charges are particularly low in Year 1 but doesn't highlight it. However, the Managing Agent and auctioneer are also parties to this deception. They could refuse, on point of principle, to become involved in such practices by insisting that estimated budgets for the following few years are also prepared and given to potential buyers.

However, there's nothing patently dishonest about this practice. The figures in the initial budget in most cases probably do, in fact, reflect the projected expenditure for Year 1 - with the exception of the lack of a sufficient Sinking Fund contribution - and there's no legal obligation to produce budgets for subsequent years.

So it's very much a case of 'caveat emptor' – let the buyer beware.

If you're considering buying a new apartment, you should see if there are projected budget figures which will indicate estimated costs for the first few years of the apartment development. If there are, it'll be very much the exception rather than the rule.

If there are no projected budgets available for future years, you should ask to see the details of the budget figures used to calculate your particular initial Service Charge. You might find it very difficult to obtain this information. If you manage to get it, you'll be able to see exactly what has been left out of the initial budget.

The annual budget

In a properly managed development, the procedures for calculating the annual budget should be as follows:

- Written quotations should be sought from the various contractors for the services to be provided for the forthcoming year.
- The Managing Agent should examine expenditure for the previous year, and the various quotations for the forthcoming year, to get the best value.
- A suitable Sinking Fund contribution should be decided by the Board of Directors.
- With all of these figures available, the Managing Agent can then prepare the budget.
- The Managing Agent and the Board of Directors should then

meet to finalise the figures.
- An informal owners' meeting should be held so that owners can discuss the figures and seek explanations from the Managing Agent on various issues. This will not be a General Meeting of the company in accordance with company law, but merely an unofficial meeting. The purpose of the meeting is to give everyone a chance to discuss the budget and voice their opinions. It also gives the company directors the opportunity, at their own discretion, to make any amendments to the budget before they formally adopt it.
- When the budget has been approved, a detailed document showing a breakdown of costings under each cost heading should be sent to the owners, along with the Service Charge invoice. Although there's no provision in the Lease in relation to this, each owner is entitled to it.

If the Managing Agent isn't prepared to follow these procedures, and the directors are unwilling to insist that he does so, there's a strong possibility that your development is not being managed properly. If that's the case the following action is open to you:

- Call an Extraordinary General Meeting (EGM) and amend the Articles of Association of the Management Company, to give the owners the authority to dismiss the Managing Agent.
- Call an EGM and insert into the Articles of Association a provision that the annual budget and Service Charge invoice must be presented to the owners in a particular format. If this resolution is passed, the Board of Directors is then legally obliged to ensure that this is done.
- Remove the directors at the next General Meeting of the company, and elect new ones.
- Refuse to pay the Service Charge until you receive an itemised budget.

Making amendments to the Articles of Association is a serious matter and you should seek legal advice before taking this action - see page 122. As mentioned elsewhere in this book, sometimes the mere threat of action is sufficient to get the desired results.

If the developer is still in control of your development, there's nothing you can do if he's not prepared to insist that the Managing Agent follow the above steps.

Budget headings

Depending on the facilities at your apartment block, a proper budget should be split into the following headings:-

Annual service contracts — These are the service contracts for all of the mechanical and electrical installations - lifts, automatic gates, fire alarms, CCTV, main water pumps, underground car park ventilation, landscaping and cleaning equipment, etc. There may also be service contracts in relation to vermin control or other maintenance issues. Each of the contracts should be itemised separately.

Cleaning — This should cover indoor and outdoor cleaning and should give details of the cleaning contracts and the frequency of cleaning. It should also cover the cost of the cleaning equipment and materials. If the Management Company employs a caretaker who does the cleaning, details should be included under a separate heading.

Landscaping — This should cover weed control, grass cutting, general maintenance and planting, and also an estimated figure to cover repair and maintenance costs of any landscaping equipment, but should not include any annual service contracts on the equipment.

Caretaker — If there's a caretaker employed by the Management Company, all costs relating to him should be itemised here.

Security — This heading is used for any costs relating to security which are not covered in any of the other sections.

Repairs and maintenance — This figure will be an estimate to cover general repairs, which aren't covered by any annual service contract, throughout the year It will include repairs to electrical or plumbing installations, doors and gates, etc. It should also include an amount for general equipment– locks, keys, bulbs, etc.

Some Managing Agents also charge a fee for visiting the apartment development at additional times or frequencies outside of those agreed in their contract. These would be unscheduled and would occur if major repair work had to be carried out and needed to be supervised, or some other unscheduled issues arise. An amount would need to be included under this heading to cover this.

General utilities These will include the electricity bills for the various installations - common area lighting, pumps, lifts, etc. - the cost of phones in the lifts, and any gas consumption. The figures should be separately itemised as much as possible.

Waste control This should cover the costs in relation to waste and domestic refuse disposal.

Insurance This should be divided into the Block Insurance - which normally includes employers' liability and property owners' liability insurance - engineering insurance and Directors' & Officers' liability insurance. There may also be other insurance headings relating to particular developments and these should also be itemised separately. See chapter 8 for further details on insurance.

Professional fees This heading should cover an estimate for professional fees in relation to audit & accountancy, company secretarial services, any Health & Safety audit, reinstatement valuation, legal fees and fire control surveys. Any project management fees should also be included here – these are fees normally paid to the Managing Agent or others for managing major planned once-off projects to be undertaken during the year, and which would not normally be included in the Managing Agent's management fee.

The Managing Agent's annual fee should not be included under this heading.

Administration This heading should cover costs such as bank charges, room hire for meetings, postage, stationery and newsletters. In

	some cases, the costs in relation to postage, stationery and newsletters are included in the overall Managing Agent's fee. It's important to clarify this with the Managing Agent before his appointment - see Appendix C.
Capital expenditure	If specific capital expenditure projects have been decided upon by the Board of Directors and aren't covered by the Sinking Fund, they should be itemised separately here.
Sinking Fund	This heading makes provision for long-term and costly redecoration, refurbishment, repairs and equipment replacement. The costings should be itemised individually as much as possible. There's more discussion on the Sinking Fund later in this chapter - see page 83.
Managing Agent's fee	This should cover the costs of the Managing Agent's annual fee as agreed with the Board of Directors - see Appendix C

Specific costings - added on or removed

There can be extra specific budget headings in the case of some apartment developments to cover additional costs only applicable to a certain section of owners. The costs relative to the additional budget headings are apportioned only among those owners who enjoy the specific benefits.

This situation is particularly relevant to car parks, in cases where only a percentage of owners have car spaces and exclusive use of the car park. Any expenses which are solely in relation to the car park should be divided among those owners - provided there's a provision for this in the Lease.

But what's the situation if the car park also contains the bike shed and bin store which will be used by all owners? Then, shouldn't everybody contribute to the car park expenses? If the car park is available to all occupiers to use, those expenses may form part of the overall annual budget and will be payable by all owners, whether they possess a car or not.

A similar position often arises with lifts. Most Leases will apportion the cost of the lift amongst all the owners in the apartment building where the lift is located, including those who have ground floor apartments and probably don't use the lift at all. No amount of protest by these owners can ever change the calculations as set out in the Lease.

The budget may also exclude certain cost headings from some owners. If you live in a development where there's a mixture of regular apartments and 'own door' duplexes, the owners of 'own door' units should not be charged for any of the costs relating to the internal common areas of the apartment buildings - internal cleaning, lift maintenance, internal electricity, decoration, etc.

This, as with all other matters, will be dictated by what's contained in your Lease. If your Lease doesn't distinguish the Service Charges, the Board of Directors isn't in a position to alter the provisions of the Lease no matter how unfair they are.

Supplemental budget

A situation can sometime arise where it's clear at some point during the financial year that the annual budget is going to fall far short of the actual expenditure. This can occur for various reasons:
- Fundamental errors in the original annual budget calculations.
- Additional significant unforeseen expenditure which wasn't envisaged when calculating the annual budget.

In such cases, the Board of Directors may decide to prepare a supplemental budget and request additional Service Charges from each owner. This decision will usually depend on the size of the anticipated budget deficit and the overall state of the Management Company's finances.

You'll probably find a provision in your Lease permitting the use of supplemental budgets. Even if there isn't, it could be argued that the production of a supplemental budget by the Board of Directors is an implied term of the Lease and good property management under the circumstances.

"My Service Charge is too high!"

You can see from the budget headings above that there can be a wide range of expenses involved in the management of your apartment development - not merely occasional cleaning, landscaping, bits and pieces of maintenance, and the block insurance. Even though you may criticise the amount of your Service Charge each year, on closer examination of the budget you just might begin to understand that your Service Charge may actually reflect the true cost of properly managing your apartment development.

If you had bought a house instead of an apartment, you'd be spending considerable money 'managing' that house each year and you should be budgeting for some, or all, of the following expenses:

- Building and property owner's liability insurance.
- Possibly the cost of a burglar alarm, and an annual maintenance contract for it.
- The cost of refuse collection.
- The cost of a gardener to cut the grass and clip the hedges.
- General repairs and replacements – glass breakage, gutters and drains, replacement of windows and external doors, gates and fences, the roof, etc.
- External painting which will need to be done every five to ten years.
- Even if you do a lot of the maintenance and gardening yourself, you'll have to buy gardening and decorating/repair equipment, and replace or repair it every few years.
- Over the years you'll probably incur expenses to upgrade the garden, perhaps put in special paving, a cobbled yard, new shrubs and plants, etc.
- There's the time it takes to actually do the gardening and maintenance - 'time is money' and this should be factored in for the purposes of making a true comparison.

I'm not attempting to say that the outlay will work out the same, but there probably isn't a huge amount in the difference. You should keep this in mind if your temperature rises every year when you receive your Service Charge invoice.

The main distinctions between the annual cost of running a house, and your Service Charge cost, are:

- If you own a house, you're in greater control of the expenditure. If your finances are getting tight or you want to take an exotic holiday this year, you can decide not to renew the gutters or paint the outside of the house, or whatever, for another year even though the job may need to be done. With an apartment you can't be selective in that way. The Board of Directors makes the decisions and you must abide by them.
- If you own a house, the expenditure is spread over a twelve month period and you don't tend to keep a running total of

everything you spend each year. With an apartment, however, you receive an invoice for the entire annual expenditure in one lump sum, and this highlights the cost in your mind, more so than if you received small invoices on a gradual basis throughout the year.
- As you can see from the budget headings above, there's considerable expenditure relating to administrative items, ranging from company law matters, audit fees, company secretarial fees and filing fees, to general management expenses, Managing Agent's fees, Health & Safety audits, reinstatement valuations, etc. These costs don't occur in relation to a standard house.

The Sinking Fund

The Sinking Fund is a type of pension fund for your development.

An apartment development is a highly multifaceted environment, usually with some very expensive and sophisticated equipment and fittings on site. Although various headings in the budget will deal with the day-to-day and annual maintenance and upkeep of the development, a proper and realistic financial plan must be put in place to cover the cost of long-term expenditure and refurbishment.

Provision must be made in the annual budget for an amount of money to be paid through the Service Charges and lodged into a separate bank account to cover these eventualities. This is known as the Sinking Fund, or the Reserve Fund.

Future expenditure on certain items should be planned ahead and adequately provided for in the Sinking Fund. These items would include:
- Major refurbishment and redecoration of the apartment buildings and common areas.
- Major structural repairs.
- The replacement of expensive equipment and fittings such as lifts, floor coverings, CCTV systems and automatic gates.

The Sinking Fund should be individually itemised as much as possible, with perhaps several deposit accounts in place so that funds put aside for lift replacement will not be spent on something else.

It's vital that if the Sinking Fund is itemised, monies are not plundered from one section to cover expenditure elsewhere. In these circumstances, a supplemental budget should be introduced instead.

There's a great temptation to make provision in the annual budget for an extremely small and, therefore, inadequate Sinking Fund, in order to keep the Service Charges low. The directors of the Management Company should never consider this option and the Managing Agent and Management Company auditor should advise them against it.

There can be a reluctance on the part of some owners to pay a contribution towards the Sinking Fund because:

- They have no confidence in the Board of Directors or Managing Agent to manage the Sinking Fund properly.
- They find it difficult to perceive the value or benefits of the Sinking Fund. Similar to insurance, it appears to them that they're paying out money but getting nothing in return for it.
- They don't intend to keep the apartment for the long term. Many owners regard their purchase of an apartment as the "first rung on the property ladder" - a short-term arrangement. They therefore don't wish to contribute to future expenses that won't be incurred for about twenty years or more, by which time they hope to be long gone from the development.

An inadequate Sinking Fund is probably the greatest problem that can face any apartment development, as it reflects on the future ability of the Board of Directors to maintain the development to a high standard. It can also affect the ability to sell an apartment and, therefore, have a negative influence on the selling price. When a second-hand apartment is being sold, one of the specific questions asked by a buyer's solicitor in the Requisitions on Title is whether or not a Sinking Fund has been put into effect, the level of the Fund and the identity of the individual or company in whose name the Fund is held.

Managing Agent's interest in contracts

Some of the larger Managing Agent companies not only carry out the overall management of developments, but also carry out a great deal of the property maintenance services themselves - either through a separate division of their own company or through companies in which they have an interest. The services in question usually involve cleaning, general maintenance and landscaping.

You should seek information on this matter from the Managing Agent or Board of Directors, either at the 'any other business' stage of the Annual General Meeting or at the informal pre-budget meeting, if one is held.

If the Managing Agent indicates that he does in fact have a financial interest in some of the contracts at the development - and there's fundamentally no harm in that - he should disclose full details to the owners. In that situation, it's essential that quotations for the particular services in question are obtained from independent contractors, as well as the Managing Agent. One of the directors of the Management Company should be appointed to oversee this process and examine the various quotations. Naturally, the contractors who best serve the needs of the development should be engaged, whether they're wholly independent or connected in some way with the Managing Agent.

Directors' interest in contracts

If any member of the Board of Directors has any financial interest in any contract with the Management Company, he's obliged under company law to inform the other directors.

Disclosure is required in the company's accounts, of all transactions with related parties and the basis of these transactions.

Payment of the Service Charge

Most Service Charges are required to be paid at the start of the Management Company's financial year. Some Managing Agents insist that they're paid in a single lump sum.

Facilities are provided by some Managing Agents whereby you can pay your Service Charge by bank standing order or direct debit, half-yearly, quarterly or monthly.

Many owners find this facility very convenient, as it spreads the Service Charge payment over the year and makes it easier to manage personal finances. You should consider this facility if it's available to you. If it's not, you should ask your Managing Agent to provide such a facility.

Some apartment Leases - particularly the older ones - state that the Service Charge is to be collected on a quarterly or half-yearly basis. If such is the case, the Directors don't have the power to alter that arrangement although there's nothing to stop any owner from paying the full Service Charge in a single lump sum at the beginning of the financial year, if they so choose.

Apportionment of the Service Charge

When the annual budget has been agreed by the Board of Directors, it's apportioned among all of the apartment owners and each portion is known as the Service Charge.

The percentage allocated to each apartment must be in accordance with each individual Lease. All of the percentages allocated throughout the development must add up to 100%.

The percentage contribution from each apartment is originally decided by the developer, often on the advice of the Managing Agent. The percentages are then inserted into each Lease. There are two main methods used to arrive at the apportionment figure for each apartment:

- The 'A/Z' method, where 'A' represents the floor area of your apartment and 'Z' represents the combined floor area of all the apartments, but not including the common areas. By this method, you pay an amount relative to the size of your apartment – the largest apartment paying the greatest percentage and the smallest apartment paying the lowest.
- The 'number of bedrooms' method. In this method, the percentages are calculated relative to the number of bedrooms in your apartment. All of the one bedroom apartments will pay a particular percentage, regardless of their individual sizes; the same with two bedroom apartments, three bedroom apartments, etc.

I've seen other methods used, particularly in very large apartment developments, the percentages being calculated on the basis of various complicated ratios.

There may also be more than one percentage figure in some Leases and this normally occurs in the following circumstances:

- When there's a mixture of apartment buildings and 'own door' units - units that don't have any internal common areas, lifts, etc., which are also known as 'duplexes'. In this situation, the apartment owners will pay a percentage of the 'internal' costs, shared only among themselves - lifts, internal cleaning, internal repairs, etc. They'll also pay a different percentage of the cost of overall management and administration of the development - management fees, insurance, landscaping, etc. These costs will be shared among all of the unit owners in the development - duplexes and apartments.
- When there's a separate car park which is only accessible to

a certain number of owners. In this case, the costs relating to the car park alone are shared among those who have access to the area, but the remaining management and administration costs are shared among all of the owners. See 'specific costs - added on or removed' on page 80.

If you decide not to pay

The collection of the annual Service Charge is probably one of the greatest headaches for Managing Agents in apartment developments.

It takes up a vast amount of time and can sap the energy and morale of both the Board of Directors and the Managing Agent.

There can be serious consequences if too many owners don't pay on time. Funds in the Management Company's bank account will eventually dry up. This will slowly cause a limiting of the essential services required to properly manage and maintain the development.

So why do owners fail or refuse to pay their Service Charge? There appear to be five principal reasons:

You can't afford it

This is an unfortunate situation which is not addressed in any Lease. The harsh reality is that if you feel that you're unlikely to be able to pay the Service Charge over a long future period, you should consider selling your apartment or not buying one in the first place.

If, however, you're going through a temporary bad financial patch, I believe that most Managing Agents would be prepared to enter into some payment arrangement with you whereby you can pay in instalments over a period of time.

If the Management Company operates a bank standing order or direct debit facility, that might also ease the burden of having to find a large single sum payment at the beginning of the financial year.

So don't be reluctant to talk with your Managing Agent if you find yourself in this situation. It's in his interest as well as yours to come to some arrangement with you.

'A matter of principle'

Maybe you're not happy with the standard of maintenance; maybe you think that the Service Charge is too high; maybe you're frustrated at the laziness of the developer in completing your development; maybe your neighbours are causing you annoyance and you feel that the issue is not being addressed properly; maybe you've some other issue about something else in your development that you feel is important, but isn't being resolved to your liking.

So what do many owners do in these circumstances?

They refuse to pay their Service Charge - in the hope and expectation that their particular grievance will be resolved.

What do you think happens when you stop paying your Service Charge because you're unhappy about the way your development is being managed? The answer is fairly obvious. The facilities and maintenance at your development will deteriorate as the Management Company's funds run out. Your development will gradually, or quickly, enter into a spiral of decline.

The phrase "cutting off your nose to spite your face" springs to mind.

The first thing you must remember if you're thinking of this course of action is that you're under a *legal duty* to pay your Service Charge. In this situation, you should pay the Service Charge and try to tackle the problems by either:

- Calling an Extraordinary General Meeting to put pressure on the Board of Directors and Managing Agent to improve the level of management.
- Getting yourself elected onto the Board of Directors at the next Annual General Meeting, so that you have a direct influence on the management of your development.

You disagree with the annual budget

As an owner and ordinary member of the Management Company, you've limited powers in the day-to-day management of your development. That task is the responsibility of the Board of Directors if the development has been handed over, or the developer if it hasn't yet been transferred.

Although I believe that it's a good idea to seek the opinions of the owners before striking the annual budget, there's no obligation on the directors, the developer or the Managing Agent to do so - unless it's enshrined in an amendment to the Articles of Association. If they're satisfied that the budget accurately reflects the level of funds needed by them to properly manage your development, you, as an ordinary company member, must accept that situation.

If you feel that there are specific aspects of the budget which are causing you serious concern - perhaps you feel that there's an element of fraud in the awarding of service contracts, or that information about the Managing Agent's, or a director's, interest in particular contracts is being withheld - you should seek legal advice on the appropriate way to challenge the budget. The issue in question would need to be exceptional and the amounts significant in order to justify taking legal action.

You just don't like paying bills

Nobody likes paying bills. Gas bills, ESB bills, insurance bills, Service Charge bills – they all arrive through our door and have to be paid.

The Irish unfortunately have a poor reputation when it comes to paying bills. There's a large body of people out there who don't believe in paying any bill until their services are about to be cut off or they're brought to court. Then, at the final hour, they'll pay up.

The legal and administration costs and cash flow problems this causes in an apartment development can be very considerable.

Boards of Directors and Managing Agents find themselves in the same position every year and it regularly becomes one of the major issues in the management of apartment developments – how to collect the Service Charge arrears to pay for the different services. The difficulties are twofold:

- If the Board of Directors is managing the development itself, without a Managing Agent, it's most likely that nobody wants to take on the task of chasing the defaulting owners for their Service Charges. It can be demoralising and hugely time-consuming and can also cause friction between neighbours.
- If the Board of Directors engages a Managing Agent, it often happens that the Managing Agent becomes disillusioned and frustrated and simply doesn't have the time required - relative to the management fee being charged - to pursue the defaulters.

Most Managing Agents are paid a flat fee for the management of the development, as agreed with the Board of Directors. If the Managing Agent finds that he needs to spend vast amounts of additional time and effort pursuing defaulting owners, he may only half-heartedly address the issue. He may realise that, if he were to devote the amount of time necessary to properly deal with the problem, he would have to increase the management fee, and the Board of Directors and owners wouldn't accept this. So, instead, some Managing Agents devote as little time as possible to the problem until it becomes a major issue.

However, much as you may not like paying bills, your Service Charge invoice is one which you *have* to pay - unless you've a very good reason for not paying, and the only reason I can think of is the lack of a breakdown of the figures.

You don't know how the figures are made up

In my opinion, you're entitled to a Service Charge invoice which gives you a clear indication as to how your Service Charge figure is calculated. I therefore believe that you're entitled to withhold payment of your Service Charge until you receive that information.

I'm referring to a situation where your Service Charge invoice is presented to you in a one-line statement, with no budget details whatsoever, either on the invoice or on an accompanying document, and in a manner whereby it's impossible for you to have any idea how the figures are calculated.

The withholding of your Service Charge is a serious matter. There's a possibility that your case might end up in court so *it's important that you seek legal advice from your solicitor before taking such action.*

Your solicitor may not agree with my opinion on the matter.

You could also seek the support of other owners and urge them to take the same action. Any legal costs should be quite manageable if all aggrieved owners use the same solicitor to deal with the matter.

If the Managing Agent refuses to provide budget details with your Service Charge invoice, it's probably because:

- He hasn't bothered to properly calculate the annual budget and is just taking a rough guess at some figures, which he wouldn't be able to justify or explain on closer examination.
- He's too overworked and just hasn't the time.
- He has something to hide.

Duty to levy and collect Service Charges

It's the legal responsibility and duty of the Board of Directors to levy and collect all Service Charges. If the directors don't do their utmost - or instruct their Managing Agent to do his utmost - to collect the Service Charges, they could be accused of negligence in the performance of their duties.

The prompt payment of Service Charges by all owners is the most fundamental and vital part of the proper management of an apartment development. I believe that not only is it the legal duty, but it's also the moral duty, of the Board of Directors to use every means within the provisions of the Lease to ensure that all Service Charges are paid promptly.

This is assuming, of course, that a copy of the annual budget on which the Service Charges are calculated was provided to each owner along with their invoice.

Service Charge arrears

During my years as a Managing Agent I devoted some considerable time to the matter of collecting Service Charge arrears. I eventually devised a method of dealing with the problem which proved to be very successful.

I established a 'Service Charge Collection Policy' for each development and I introduced this procedure with the approval of the various Boards of Directors.

There's only one drawback to this procedure. There's a question-mark over whether or not it's within the legalities of the Lease to use step 4 - the removal of the defaulter and his lending institution as interested parties from the insurance policy. Please refer to step 4 below for further discussion of this matter.

The other steps of the procedure, however, are well within the power and authority of the Board of Directors.

I would advise that if you're a director of a Management Company and wish to introduce these procedures, you should first seek advice, in writing, from the Management Company's solicitor or Managing Agent. You then must weigh up the risk of the Management Company being taken to court, against the prospect of a situation where every owner pays his Service Charge on time, every year.

If you're an owner and would like to see these procedures implemented, you should contact your Board of Directors or Managing Agent and discuss the matter with them. You could then raise the matter under 'any other business' at the Annual General Meeting to see what other owners think of the idea.

Administration fees

Most modern apartment Leases have a provision which states very clearly that the owner is liable for any costs or outlay which occurs, consequent on his breach or non compliance with the terms of the Lease. See page 55.

Failure to pay the Service Charge would certainly constitute a breach of the Lease and, therefore, it seems clear to me that, any costs or expenses reasonably incurred while pursuing the defaulters for the Service Charge arrears, must be charged to those specific owners.

If such a provision is not expressly included in the Lease, I believe that it could be argued successfully that it's an implied term of the Lease, and therefore the Managing Agent is entitled to levy the costs and outlays against the relevant owners.

These 'administration fees' should be levied for any actions whatsoever taken by the Managing Agent to collect the Service Charge once it becomes overdue, and therefore a breach of the Lease has occurred.

The amount of the administration fee to be imposed is a matter for each Board of Directors and Managing Agent to decide. The main point to remember is that it shouldn't be too low - or else it's not a sufficient deterrent to the defaulter, and it shouldn't be too high - or else it might appear unreasonably punitive.

In my opinion, and in order to comply with the Lease, the administration fee should be paid to whoever carries out the additional work in chasing the overdue Service Charges. If the task is undertaken by the Managing Agent, he should receive the additional fees - in that case VAT would also have to be charged. If the Board of Directors undertakes the work, it should receive the fees. This matter must clarified by the directors before this procedure is implemented.

Service Charge Collection Policy

I received many threats from owners and their solicitors to the effect that they would take me to court if I proceeded with this procedure against them. I always considered, however, that the prompt payment of the Service Charges was such a fundamental cornerstone in the proper management of each apartment development that it was worth taking the risk.

Nobody ever followed up on the threat.

I would also like to point out that this procedure should not be adopted in cases where there's a genuine dispute with an owner, but only where the dispute is *in relation to the Service Charge itself.* If there's a dispute with an owner in relation to any other matter at the development, and he's refusing to pay his Service Charge until the dispute is resolved, I'd inform him that he's not entitled to withhold the Service Charges under those circumstances, and I'd commence the procedure against him.

Here are the various steps I took when acting as a Managing Agent, to encourage prompt payment of Service Charges.

Step 1 - Documents to the owners

The Service Charge invoice is sent to each owner, showing clearly the date on which the money is due. As discussed earlier a copy of the annual budget on which the Service Charge is based, showing a breakdown of the budget costings and headings, should accompany the invoice, together with any additional explanatory information.

You should also include a copy of the 'Service Charge Collection Policy explanatory document' which should outline clearly the various actions and charges which will occur if the Service Charge is not paid by the due date. See Appendix G for a typical example of such a document.

Step 2 – Impose interest

Most Leases contain a clause whereby interest must be levied on any owner's Service Charge account which is in arrears, until such time as all outstanding sums are paid. The specific interest rate to be charged will also be outlined in the Lease.

Within two weeks following the due date for the payment of the Service Charge, a copy invoice with a letter stating that the Service Charge is now overdue is sent to each owner who has not yet paid, along with details of the interest and the administration fee being charged. The administration fee is added to the defaulting owner's account, and should be shown on the owner's financial statement.

I would also send a further copy of the 'Service Charge Collection Policy explanatory document' to the defaulters, so that they're fully aware of the further action which will be taken against them if they continue to default on their payment.

The Managing Agent now applies interest to the overdue accounts. The Board of Directors is legally obliged to ensure that this is done if there's such an interest provision in the Lease. The Managing Agent should have computer accounts programs which can automatically apply interest to the relevant accounts.

Step 3 – Further communication with the defaulters

If the Service Charge remains unpaid for a further period of time - the period of time as decided by the directors and outlined in the policy document - a robust reminder letter is sent to the defaulters. This letter should state that the Service Charge, together with any fees and interest, must be paid immediately and that, if not paid within a further specific period of time, the next step in the procedure would be implemented – the removal of the defaulter and his lending institution, if any, as 'interested parties' from the block insurance policy.

A further administration fee should be charged to the defaulter to cover the cost of sending this reminder letter.

With this letter, I'd also send a copy of the Service Charge invoice and statement, showing the accumulating interest charges and administration fees, and another copy of the 'Service Charge Collection Policy explanatory document', so that the defaulter can be left in no doubt about what will happen next.

Step 4 – Removal from the insurances

This is the most controversial aspect of my 'Service Charge Collection Policy'.

If, having exhausted steps 1, 2 and 3, some of the owners still haven't paid their Service Charge - and this will no doubt be the case - this is the final option available to the Managing Agent before going to court.

The Managing Agent instructs the insurance broker to remove the name of the defaulter, and that of his lending institution, as 'interested parties' from the block insurance policy. A letter is sent to the defaulting owner and the lending institution to state that this action has been taken.

On what basis can the Managing Agent take this action?

There's a provision in every Lease to the effect that the Board of Directors is under no obligation to provide *any* services to an owner, if the owner's Service Charges are in arrears. One of the services provided by the Board of Directors under the Lease is to arrange appropriate insurance cover on behalf of the owners, and to ensure that the insurance broker notes each owner and their lending institution, if any, as interested parties, on the insurance policy.

Every lending institution insists on being registered as an interested party on the block insurance policy. It's an important legal condition of the mortgage and a pre-requisite to obtaining the loan. The reason for this is that they wish to protect their asset. If the block insurance policy is about to lapse or be cancelled for some reason, the lending institution must be informed by the insurance company - but only if it's registered as an interested party on the policy. This is why it insists on being registered as an interested party.

The removal of a defaulter and his lending institution as interested parties doesn't mean that the defaulter is no longer insured under the policy, because the block insurances pertain to all of the apartment buildings and individual apartments, as a whole. The real effect of this action is in relation to the lending institution.

The lending institutions become extremely concerned when they're removed as interested parties from the block insurance.

I don't know what action they take in relation to the borrower - the defaulting owner - but I've observed Service Charge payments coming in very quickly following this action, either from the borrower or sometimes from the lending institution itself.

Have the directors the power to sanction this action under the provisions of the Lease? It's a debatable point. Although the directors don't have to provide any services for a defaulting owner, do they have the right to reverse a service they've *already* provided - the service of recording the owner's and lending institution's interest on the insurance policy? This point is uncertain and will eventually have to be decided by a judge, if it ever gets that far.

There are some other points which I'd like to make in relation to this action:

- It's interesting to note that no lending institution ever approached me and queried the directors' right to remove them as interested parties from the insurance policy.
- If an owner wishes to challenge his removal from the insurance policy he must seek an injunction to restrain the directors from taking this action. Such a case must be taken in the Circuit Court. In most cases the legal cost to him of taking this case will far exceed the amount of Service Charges which he owes.
- If he decides to proceed in the Circuit Court, there's no guarantee that he'd win. He's taking a big chance, seeking relief against the Management Company in a court, while, at the same time, owing money to that Management Company.
- If the court feels that the owner is entitled to an injunction stopping the directors from removing him as an interested party, he may not receive his legal costs if the judge is sympathetic towards the Management Company. Or the costs may be offset against the Service Charge arrears.

The chances are that the defaulting owner will pay up rather than take the matter to the Circuit Court, but the directors and Managing Agent must be aware that they run a risk that they may become involved as defendants in a Circuit Court action. It may require some courage on their part.

However, in my opinion, if there's a regime of persistent non-payment of Service Charges in your development, that risk may very well be worth taking, in order to send a warning to the defaulters that the Board of Directors and Managing Agent are determined to clean up the situation of non-payment of Service Charges.

There are some further points I'd like to mention before proceeding to step 5:

There's quite an amount of administrative work involved:

- The removal of the defaulter and his lending institution, as interested parties, off the insurance policy.
- Communications to the defaulter, his lending institution and the insurance broker.
- The reinstatement of the defaulter and lending institution as interested parties when the arrears have been paid.

Therefore, an appropriate administration fee should be levied accordingly and the defaulter should be informed about this.

The effect of this particular step will be considerably weakened if the defaulter doesn't have a lending institution.

If the Board of Directors isn't prepared to take the risk of proceeding with step 4, it can jump from step 3 directly to step 5.

Step 5 – Legal proceedings

If, by this time, the defaulter still hasn't paid the Service Charge, a formal notice should be sent by the Management Company's solicitor to the owner *and his lending institution* stating that legal proceedings would be taken against him for forfeiture of his Lease, if the arrears were not paid within 28 days. If there's no response to this notice - and the lending institution will almost certainly take action at this stage - legal proceedings should immediately be issued in the Circuit Court against the owner, for:

- Forfeiture of his Lease.
- Damages.
- Costs.

I'd also state in a letter to the owner accompanying the notice, that the owner has already incurred legal costs for which he's liable, and that these costs will increase considerably if he allows a Circuit Court summons to be issued against him.

This legal claim shouldn't merely be for the payment of a contract debt - the Service Charge arrears. It should be for forfeiture of the Lease. Under the terms of the Lease, the Board of Directors is entitled to seek this relief. Such a case must be taken in the Circuit Court, as it's much more serious than a contract debt. While it's accepted that it's unlikely that the court will grant the forfeiture of the Lease, it can award damages far and above the amount of the Service Charge arrears. This will depend on the circumstances of the case. Legal costs will also be awarded, under normal circumstances, against the defaulting owner, and these could be considerable.

Apart from the costs awarded in favour of the Management Company, there may be some 'solicitor and client' costs which the Management

Company must pay to its own solicitor. Under the terms of the Lease, these can be charged to the defaulting owner as additional administration fees incurred following on his breach of the terms of the Lease.

In my opinion, this legal action should be arrived at no later than four months after the Service Charge was due for payment, so that the owner is aware that the directors aren't going to drag their heels on the issue, and that he'll be stubbornly pursued until he pays that which is owed to the Management Company – his Service Charges.

Legal proceedings require the production of all sorts of documentation and there's quite a lot of administration involved. I would suggest, therefore, that the Management Company's solicitor should be instructed to include a further administration fee in the court claim. In my opinion, a court would look favourably on such a fee if the amount is reasonable.

Conclusion

If the Board of Directors implements such a 'Service Charge Collection Policy' and the Managing Agent is efficient in administering it, the following should be the effect:

- If the owners are aware that there's a strict 'Service Charge Collection Policy' in place, and that it'll be implemented on a resolute and efficient basis against all defaulters, the number of defaulters will decrease considerably each year.
- The compliant owners will have more confidence in their Board of Directors and Managing Agent, and more trust in their ability to properly manage the development.
- The Managing Agent in turn will have more time to get on with the task of managing the development, without spending unnecessary effort and countless hours chasing the Service Charges and trying to manage the various expenditures with insufficient funds.

Service Charge arrears in a new development

The procedures are slightly different if the developer hasn't handed over the development to the Management Company. In such a case, the developer, as Lessor, is legally responsible for all aspects of the management of the development including the collection of Service Charges.

The approval of the developer should be sought before a Managing Agent introduces a 'Service Charge Collection Policy' as outlined above.

It also appears that any legal proceedings taken against defaulters would have to be taken in the name of the developer, as the Management Company has no legal authority on such matters at this stage.

The Managing Agent must take his instructions from the developer, even if there's an 'ad hoc' committee in place - see page 13.

It's unclear as to the remedies open to the owners or Managing Agent if the developer decides not to allow legal proceedings be taken in his name against defaulters. It could be argued that the owners, as Lessees, could take legal action against the developer for breaches of his covenant, contained in the Lease, to levy and collect the Service Charges.

Service Charge arrears when selling an apartment

A Service Charge debt attaches to the apartment and the owner *for the time being* of that apartment. If an owner is in arrears when selling his apartment, the buyer's solicitor will insist that all Service Charge arrears be paid before the sale can be completed.

If you're buying an apartment which has Service Charge arrears attached to it, the amount of those arrears should be deducted from the purchase price which the seller was due to receive, and should be paid directly to the Management Company. This means that you'll be starting as the new owner with a 'clean slate'.

If you bought a second-hand apartment and there were Service Charge arrears which weren't settled at the time of the sale, the Board of Directors is legally bound to demand the arrears from you - the Service Charge arrears attach to the apartment and to the owner of the apartment, and you're now the owner.

In this situation, you should contact the solicitor who acted for you when you bought the apartment. He would have been responsible to ensure that all arrears were paid out of the purchase price. If he failed or neglected to do this, I believe that he should pay the arrears himself, and seek to recover them from the vendor of the apartment.

If your solicitor refuses to take any action, you need to consult another solicitor or the Law Society of Ireland.

Voting rights of owners in arrears

The Articles of Association of the Management Company will state that no member is entitled to vote at any General Meeting of the company if they owe any money to the company.

Therefore, *if you're in arrears with your Service Charges, you can't vote at Annual General Meetings or Extraordinary General Meetings of the Management Company.* You are, however, entitled to attend the meetings.

The chairman of any General Meeting of the Management Company should check that all those who are voting on any resolution are not in arrears with their Service Charges and are, therefore, eligible to vote.

Many apartment owners aren't aware of this rule. In my opinion, it would be a good idea to send out a note about this rule to all owners whenever a General Meeting - Annual or Extraordinary - is being called. If there are controversial resolutions to be discussed and voted on at the meeting, you might find some owners quickly paying their Service Charge arrears in order to be able to cast their vote.

If you're attending a General Meeting of the company, and feel that there are owners voting at the meeting who may have Service Charge arrears, you should bring it to the attention of the chairman of the meeting. You can't query the outcome of a vote on that basis after the meeting has finished - see also page 108.

The first bank account

As soon as the first apartment is sold, the apartment development changes from being a building site under the control of the developer, into a 'managed property' under the control of the developer.

The Management Company's bank account sometimes becomes 'live' at this time and the Service Charges received by the developer's solicitor on sale closings are lodged into it. In some cases the funds are controlled through an account held by the Managing Agent.

This is a situation where practicality is used, rather than the precise legal formalities. At this time it's the developer - as the Lessor - who is managing the development under the terms of the Lease, until such time as he hands it over to the Management Company. Strictly speaking, all Service Charges should therefore be paid into an account controlled by the developer, and all management services should be paid for out of that account.

The Management Company's bank account should not become operational until such time as the developer's interests and responsibilities are transferred to the Management Company, and it takes over the responsibility to manage the development.

Most developers are quite happy to allow the Management Company account to operate to control the management expenses of the development. They'd prefer not to have anything to do with the receipt of the Service Charges.

The control of the bank accounts

Once the developer has handed over the development, all matters in relation to the Management Company, including the bank accounts, are under the control of the Board of Directors.

Where there's a Managing Agent engaged, the question of the authorised signatures on the cheque books must be decided by the directors.

Sinking Fund account: In my opinion, the Board of Directors should maintain total control over the Sinking Fund bank account. The Managing Agent shouldn't be an authorised signature on that account. As the funds in the Sinking Fund account should only be accessed in specific circumstances, the Board of Directors should be directly involved in authorising any withdrawals from that account.

General current account: All payments in relation to the day-to-day running of the development will be made by the Managing Agent, on behalf of the Management Company. It's not unreasonable, therefore, for the Managing Agent to insist that he's one of the authorised signatures on the account, along with one or two of the directors. The mandate to the bank should be that 'any one' of the authorised signatures can sign, so that the Managing Agent can pay bills without having to find a director to countersign every time.

If the Board of Directors doesn't have enough confidence in the Managing Agent to allow him to sign cheques to pay for the management of the development, it may be time to consider changing the Managing Agent.

Service Charge apportionment – Years 1 & 2

In all of the apartment developments which I've dealt with, the financial year has commenced on the first day of the month in which the first apartment sale takes place, and the financial year of the Management Company has followed accordingly.

This is the month when the development transforms from being a mere building site into a managed property, even if there's only one apartment sold and occupied.

So we're in Year 1 - the first year of the 'life' of a new development. A budget was prepared by the developer. All the buyers are paying their first year's Service Charge along with the purchase price. For the sake of illustration, let's say that the first apartment was sold sometime in January. The financial year for the development, therefore, will run from January to December each year.

And let's say that you bought your apartment in this development on April 1st - a quarter way into the financial year. You'll be asked to pay the full annual Service Charge on sale closing. This Service Charge covers the full financial year, even though you should only be paying for three-quarters of it.

At the end of Year 1 a 'credit forward' will be applied to your Service Charge account for Year 2. The amount credited forward will be for the number of days in Year 1's financial year, when you didn't own your apartment.

In the example given above, the sum credited forward into Year 2 will be a quarter of the Service Charge that you paid in Year 1 – you didn't own the apartment for a quarter of that financial year, so you won't be expected to pay any Service Charge for that period.

The credit forward will be credited to your Service Charge invoice in Year 2 and that invoice will be amended accordingly. This, however, will lead to a shortfall in funds in Year 2.

A more simple way to deal with the matter would be for the solicitors to calculate the portion of the Service Charge which you owe from sale closing until the end of the financial year, and you only pay that amount when you sign your Lease. I'm not aware of any development where this method is used.

The 'missing' Service Charges

If we stay with the above example we see that you received your credit forward in Year 2 for that portion of Year 1 - January to April - when you didn't own your apartment.

During that period between January and April some of the apartments were occupied, the development was being managed and expenses were being incurred - insurance, electricity, cleaning, management fees, etc. It's quite obvious that you shouldn't have to pay for expenses incurred in that period because you didn't own your apartment - that's why you get your credit forward in Year 2. Other buyers will also be receiving credits forward in Year 2, depending on the date on which they bought their apartment in Year 1.

However, the budget and Service Charges were originally calculated on the basis that every apartment pays its share *for the full year* and that the total sum of all the Service Charges will be equal to the budget figure.

So who should pay for the periods in Year 1 when some of the apartments in the development were unsold? Is the developer obliged to pay? There's no definite answer to this, and there's no provisions in any Lease to deal with the issue. According to Leases, Service Charges don't arise until an apartment is sold.

This can cause quite a headache for Managing Agents, particularly when there's a shortfall in the accounts in Years 1 and 2 and the developer refuses to make any contribution.

Annual accounts and audit

Every limited liability company is obliged under company law to keep proper books of accounts in relation to all receipts and expenditures of the company. The procedures and finer details are to be found in various company regulations, and also in the Articles of Association of the company.

The process of preparing and filing the Annual Return is usually handled by either the company secretary or the auditor.

The annual accounts must be approved by the owners at the Annual General Meeting. When approved at the AGM, the accounts form part of the Annual Return to the Companies Office.

The auditor will provide a report when submitting the annual accounts to the owners at the AGM. If he's happy with the state of the company's books and the information he received in order to complete the audit, his report will state this. If, however, he isn't happy with the situation, or if he didn't receive all the information which he needed, he must say so in his report. Accounts which contain such a report are known as "qualified accounts".

Copies of the accounts along with the directors' and auditor's reports must be sent to every member at least 21 days before the date of the AGM.

The Management Company, like all other limited liability companies, must file an Annual Return with the Registrar of Companies every year. There are strict time limits for the filing of the Annual Return, and heavy penalties are imposed if it isn't filed within those time limits.

This matter is of critical importance for your apartment development. If the Annual Return isn't filed, the company will initially face heavy fines, and will eventually be struck off the Register of Companies. This will have serious consequences for all owners - see page 124.

However, as with all other compliance matters, it's the Board of Directors which ultimately carries the responsibility to ensure that the Management Company is compliant with company law.

A small number of Management Companies have been incorporated as 'companies limited by shares'. Most small companies limited by shares can avail of certain audit exemptions. They lose this exemption if they fail to file the Annual Return on time.

Access to company books

Directors' access: I'm aware of cases where Managing Agents have refused, for some reason, to hand over important company documents, including books of account, to the directors. A Managing Agent isn't entitled under any circumstances to deny the Board of Directors access to any of the company documents or accounts records. If your Managing Agent is acting in this way, you should instruct the Management Company's solicitor to send a strongly worded letter to him, and that'll probably resolve the situation.

Members' access: Members of a company don't have the automatic right to inspect the company's books of account. The Articles of Association of the company can be amended by the owners to permit such a right.

Private 'gated' developments

There are a few differences between an apartment development and a private 'gated' development in relation to financial matters.

The annual budget will be a little simpler in a private 'gated' development, due to the fact that some of the cost headings won't exist - such as internal cleaning and repairs, lifts, buildings insurance, etc.

However, most of the other headings will still be relevant. The sums involved should be considerably less in relation to the Sinking Fund, repairs, management fees, annual maintenance contracts, etc., but they'll still be there.

All the administration costs involved in operating an apartment development are also relevant in the operation of a private 'gated' development - company law must be complied with, proper books of account must be kept, Service Charges must be collected, landscapers and other contractors engaged, etc.

It can be a source of great frustration to house owners in such a development to realise that a large portion of the annual budget goes towards the administration of the Management Company, and not the actual provision of the various services.

The 'Service Charge Collection Policy' outlined above can also be implemented. You can't, however, remove a defaulting owner and his lending institution from the block insurance policy, because there isn't one. Each house in such a development is normally insured separately by each owner.

If you're considering buying a house *in a mixed development of houses and apartment blocks,* you should check carefully that you're not also contributing through your Service Charge for some of the services required only by the apartment blocks - internal cleaning and repairs, lift maintenance, etc.

Summary

◄ The annual budget should be presented, along with the Service Charge invoice, to all owners, in a clear and comprehensive manner.

◄ Owners are entitled to be informed if any director of the Management Company or the Managing Agent has any financial or other interest in any of the service contracts pertaining to the development.

◄ It's the responsibility of the Board of Directors to approve the budget and ensure that it's adequate for the proper maintenance of the development.

◄ The annual budget, in the first few years of a development, can be quite misleading as several of the cost headings may not arise until later years.

◄ Each owner has contracted in the Lease to pay the Service Charge each year within the required time frame, and they're absolutely liable to do so.

◄ It's the responsibility of the Board of Directors to pursue all owners who fail to pay the Service Charge on time.

◄ Owners who are in arrears with their Service Charges are not entitled to vote at General Meetings of the Management Company.

◄ The Board of Directors must ensure that proper records of receipts and expenditure are kept, and that a set of annual accounts is prepared and approved at the Annual General Meeting of the Management Company, and filed with the Annual Return, on time, in the Companies Office.

Chapter 7

Legal Matters

When you buy an apartment, you become part of a complex legal structure - a 'communal legal relationship', whereby:
- You've a property interest in your own apartment - a long leasehold interest - and a property interest in various rights-of-way within the development.
- You've a property interest in the common areas. You're a joint owner of them along with the other apartment owners, by virtue of your membership of the Management Company, which owns them.
- You've an interest in the reversion of all of the apartments to the Management Company - when the Leases expire hundreds of years away - by virtue of your membership of that company.

Limited company legal issues

The legal structure of an apartment development is founded on the concept of the limited liability company. Apart from very few exceptions, all apartment development 'communities' are formed into limited liability companies - the typical Management Company.

There are various forms of limited liability company available but most apartment developments are structured on either 'companies limited by shares' or 'companies limited by guarantee'. From your point of view, as an owner, there's no significant difference between the two types of company. There are certain differences from the Board of Director's and company secretary's point of view in relation to legal and accounting formalities. The Management Company's auditor and solicitor can advise them in that regard.

The limited liability company is a two-tiered structure consisting of the members, and the directors they appoint at General Meetings of the company.

Regardless of the type of company involved, you become a member of that company when you buy your apartment. You're also entitled to put yourself forward for election onto the Board of Directors.

Registered office

Every limited company must have a registered office - an address where all official communications can be sent, and where the company registers and company seal should be kept. Any address within the State can be used.

Shortcomings of the company structure

Before going into the complexities of corporate governance, company law and compliance regulations, I can hear many owners asking, "why do we need a company structure to run our apartment block?"

I suppose the simple answer to that question is, "because that's the way it has always been done".

In my opinion, the company environment isn't particularly suitable to the management of apartment developments, and this structure is now beginning to cause problems in Ireland. Government departments and other agencies are examining this issue.

The concept behind the company structure is that the liability of each member is limited in the event of the company going into liquidation, or ceasing to trade and owing large sums of money to creditors. In my opinion, that concept is completely irrelevant in relation to Management Companies. Limited liability companies were designed for commercial trading needs, and don't satisfy the requirements of apartment owners.

However, at the time of writing, we're stuck with the company structures. As an owner of an apartment - and therefore a member of the Management Company - it's important that you're fully aware of the workings of your company's structure, and of your duties and rights under that structure.

If you're on the Board of Directors it's absolutely vital that you've a thorough understanding of these matters. Company law and the courts presume that you have.

Memorandum & Articles of Association

Every limited liability company is founded on a document known as 'The Memorandum & Articles of Association'. These are the rules under which the company operates - the constitution of the company.

The Memorandum of Association defines the types of activities which the company was established to undertake - the 'business' of the company. The company must stay within those limitations. These vary from company to company, and will be pretty straightforward for your Management Company.

The Articles of Association, in conjunction with company law, sets out how the company is structured, how it goes about its business, and how it regulates itself. The main issues dealt with in the Articles of Association relate to:

- Duties and rights of the company members - the owners.
- Duties and powers of the company directors.
- Election and dismissal of the directors.
- Convening of company General Meetings and regulations surrounding them.
- Voting rights of the members.
- Matters in relation to the annual accounts.
- Amendment of the Articles of Association.

Your solicitor would have obtained a copy of the Memorandum & Articles of Association of the Management Company when you were buying your apartment. You won't need to spend much time examining the Memorandum of Association. The activities and 'business' of the Management Company are quite specific and will be clearly defined.

However, as a member of the company, you should be aware of the contents of the Articles of Association because you'll need that information to understand more clearly the workings of your Management Company, and the legal procedures open to you if you feel that the company is not being run in a satisfactory manner.

Members of the company

When you buy your apartment you'll sign, among other things, a document which will cause you to become a member of the Management Company. Your name will be entered in the Register of Members.

As a member of the company, you can:

- Attend all General Meetings of the company.
- Elect and dismiss directors, approve the annual accounts and vote on other resolutions, provided your Service Charges are not in arrears.
- You can also appoint somebody else to attend any meeting and vote on your behalf - called a 'proxy vote'.

- Put yourself forward to become a director of the company.
- Call an Extraordinary General Meeting of the company.
- Seek amendments to the Memorandum & Articles of Association of the Company.
- Apply to the Director of Corporate Enforcement or the High Court for redress where the company, or any of its officers, are in breach of the rules or procedures as set out in the Articles of Association or company law. I won't elaborate on this issue any further here, except to suggest that you should seek legal advise if you wish to take such action.

You'll notice that there's one thing not mentioned in the above list – the actual management of the business of company. As an apartment owner and member of the Management Company, you've very little control or management of the day-to-day operations of the Management Company as it goes about the business of managing your development.

Your only method of control is your voting right at General Meetings of the company, in particular your right to dismiss and appoint directors, and your right to amend the Articles of Association. Owners can give themselves more influence in the management of the development by amending the Articles of Association - see page 122.

Register of members

A register of members must be kept at the registered office of the company and it must include the following:

- Members' names.
- Members' addresses.
- Number of shares held by each member, if relevant.
- Date when the member became a member - ie. bought the apartment.
- Date when the member ceased to be a member - ie. sold the apartment.

This register is available for inspection by any member of the public.

Voting at General Meetings

Every owner is entitled to vote on resolutions put forward at Annual General Meetings or Extraordinary General Meetings of the Management Company - provided they're not in arrears with their Service Charges.

It's not always the case of 'one owner - one vote' The voting rights, or 'weight' of each owner's vote, will be outlined in the Articles of Association, and will usually consist of one of these situations:
- Each owner has one vote regardless of the number of apartments they own.
- Each owner has one vote for each apartment which they own.
- The percentage value of each member's vote is directly related to the percentage of the annual budget which that owner's Service Charge represents. This situation is quite rare.

The original subscribers to the Memorandum & Articles of Association of the Company - the developer's nominees - also have voting rights - see below.

If you're unhappy with any of the above voting methods, you can seek to have the Articles of Association amended at a General Meeting of the company and this can be done under the provisions of those same Articles of Association.

The developer's majority vote

At the initial stages of your development, the developer establishes the Management Company and he nominates a list of subscribers to the company. These subscribers wouldn't be apartment owners - at that stage there wouldn't be any apartments - but they'd be colleagues or business contacts of the developer.

In some Articles of Association of Management Companies, these subscribers have 'weighted' voting rights, which they'll use in favour of the developer. In these cases, there's a provision included in the section on voting rights to say that all members of the company have one vote each, *with the exception that each of the subscribers to the Memorandum & Articles of Association has 100 votes each.* It may not be 100 - it could be 50, or 200, or some other number. Whatever the number, you can be sure that the subscribers will be able to 'outweigh' the combined total of all the owners' votes.

In this way, the developer can maintain total control over the workings of the Management Company until such time as he's ready to transfer his interests and responsibilities to the owners, and walk away from your development. When this time arrives his nominees will resign as company directors and subscriber-members, and won't make themselves available for re-election.

These weighted voting rights can turn out to be very unfair on apartment owners, particularly in cases where the developer is slow to transfer the development to the owners and, therefore, maintains control for many years after the development has been finished.

It can effectively exclude owners from becoming directors of the Management Company, or effecting changes to the Articles of Association - even many years after the development has been finished - because the subscribers will always be able to out-vote the owners. It could be argued that there may be legal procedures available through the courts to redress this situation in certain circumstances, particularly in relation to the illegal or unfair suppression of minority rights. You should contact your solicitor if you wish to pursue this possibility.

Not all Articles of Association contain this voting advantage in favour of the subscribers.

Company directors

Board of Directors

Every limited liability company must have a Board of Directors, and you'll find that your Management Company has one. Under the provisions of company law, there must be a minimum of two directors.

At the initial stages of an apartment development, the developer establishes the Management Company and nominates the first directors.

When the developer eventually hands over his interests and responsibilities to the owners of the development, they'll elect their own Board of Directors usually from among the owners themselves - although a non-member of the company can be elected a director of the company if the Articles of Association permit it.

The primary function of the Board of Directors is to manage the company on behalf of the members. Under company law and the Memorandum & Articles of Association of the company, it's the legal duty of the directors to competently manage the affairs of the company, and this normally falls into two categories:

- Manage the 'business' of the company – to manage and maintain all aspects of the apartment development.
- Manage the affairs of the Management Company – to ensure that the company complies with company law.

It's the Board of Directors, collectively and individually, that has these obligations – not you as a company member.

Director as 'Fiduciary'

A director is in a unique position in relation to the company.

He must at all times act as a fiduciary – a person in a position of absolute trust. This means that he's required to act in a manner which places the interests of the company ahead of his own. Each director also has a legal duty to place the interests of the company before the interests of members, creditors or employees.

Boards of Directors of Management Companies, unfortunately, don't always act primarily in the best interests of the company. As the directors are also apartment owners, there's often a conflict of interest and they sometimes make decisions in the interest of their property ownership, rather than in the broader interest of the Management Company.

Duties of directors

The duties of company directors are considerably onerous under company law, and the manner in which they exercise those duties is a complex issue.

Company law presumes that every company director is fully aware of the legal obligations and powers relating to his office. There's no exception made for Management Companies, where the directors are for the most part inexperienced, non-professional and voluntary individuals who find themselves - often reluctantly - in the position of company director, purely by virtue of the fact they own an apartment and would like a say in how their development is managed. This is another reason why I feel that the company structure isn't a suitable basis for the management of apartment developments.

The duties of company directors are many and varied:

- Their most fundamental responsibility is to manage the 'business' of the company with due care, skill and diligence and they can be held liable if they act in a reckless or negligent manner - the main 'business' of the company is to properly and competently manage the apartment development.
- They must manage the business in accordance with the Memorandum & Articles of Association, and company law.
- They must act in good faith and primarily in the best interests of the company itself, even if this conflicts with their own interests or the interests of the members.
- They must, as officers of the company, comply with all their

legal duties under company law, and ensure that the company is also compliant in all legal and revenue matters.
- They must ensure that the correct checks and controls are in place to safeguard the assets of the Management Company.
- They must ensure that proper books of account are kept by the company in accordance with company law.
- They must ensure that the annual accounts are prepared and that an annual audit is performed in accordance with company law. Companies limited by shares can avail of certain audit exemptions.
- They have a duty to maintain certain company registers containing essential information about the company, its members and directors.
- They must divulge to the Board of Directors any interest which they have in any contract or proposed contract to be entered into by the company.
- They must convene any General Meetings of the company - Annual General Meetings and Extraordinary General Meetings - within the timeframe, and in a manner, as set down by company law and the Articles of Association of the company.
- They must ensure that minutes are taken of all directors' meetings, and retained by the company secretary. The Director of Corporate Enforcement is entitled to inspect these minutes.

The directors have the right and power to delegate the operation of the above functions to qualified and competent individuals and contractors such as Managing Agents, auditors, company secretaries, etc. They must take all reasonable steps to ensure that the contractor or individual is properly qualified, skilled and adequately insured to undertake the task. They can be held liable to the owners if they don't take these steps and something goes wrong.

Penalties and sanctions against directors

Where directors of a company fail to comply with company law they may be guilty of a criminal offence and may be liable to fines and/or imprisonment.

A court also has the discretion to disqualify a person from holding directorships in any company for a period of time if the director, while acting as a director, has been guilty of:
- Fraud in relation to a company or its members.
- A breach of his duty as director of a company.

- Conduct which renders him unfit in the eyes of the court to manage a company.
- Two or more offences of failing to maintain proper books of account.
- Three or more omissions under the Companies Acts.

Application to the courts for any of the above sanctions or penalties is usually made by the Director of Corporate Enforcement, following complaints from members of the company, creditors, etc.

As already mentioned the courts won't take into account the fact that you're not an experienced director, or that you're acting in a voluntary capacity.

There may also be further implications for directors of the Management Company if they hold office in other companies. The Director of Corporate Enforcement may decide to inspect these other companies for compliance, arising from any non-compliance of the Management Company.

Civil liability of directors

If you're a director of the Management Company, you're also liable to be sued in the civil courts if you perform your functions as a director in a negligent or reckless manner, whereby damage is caused to another person. This is in addition to the sanctions and penalties which may be imposed by the courts for your failure to properly discharge your functions as a company director.

As a director of the Management Company, you owe a duty of care to all owners and visitors to the apartment block. The main duties are:

- To competently and properly manage all aspects of the apartment development and maintain it as a safe environment.
- To ensure that the development is adequately insured.
- To make provision for an adequate Sinking Fund.
- To comply with all Health & Safety, and company law regulations
- To check out the credentials of all contractors who work in the development, particularly with regard to competency and insurance. This duty can be delegated to the Managing Agent, but you must also check out the competency and insurances of the Managing Agent before his appointment - see Appendix C.

If, while acting as a director, you're negligent or reckless in the way you deal with any of the above issues you might be personally exposed to legal proceedings for damages taken by any person - usually an owner - who feels that he has suffered a loss, due to your negligence or recklessness.

Here are a few illustrations of this point:

- When is the last time a reinstatement valuation was carried out at your development for the purposes of an accurate insurance figure? What if there's a significant insurance claim and the development isn't adequately insured, and the owners have to make up the shortfall? Who'll be blamed? The directors.
- What if the Sinking Fund hasn't been adequately maintained over the years, and is insufficient to cover essential foreseen major replacements and repairs? Who'll be blamed? The directors.
- What if there's a fire in the apartment building, and people are injured or killed because the emergency exit doors were locked or blocked. Who'll be blamed? The directors.
- What if the Managing Agent turns out to be grossly incompetent, thereby causing the values of the apartments to fall because the development is in a state of disrepair? Who'll be blamed? Ultimately, the directors.
- What if the Managing Agent doesn't have professional indemnity insurance, and, by his direct actions or inactions, there's damage done in the development? Who'll be blamed? Ultimately, the directors.
- What if the Managing Agent doesn't have a financial bonding arrangement in place, and he misappropriates Service Charge funds and/or the Sinking Fund? Who'll be blamed? Ultimately, the directors.
- What if the Annual Return isn't made to the Companies Office, and the Management Company is struck off the Register of Companies, whereby no owner can sell his apartment? Who'll be blamed? Ultimately, the directors.
- What if the annual budget is regularly struck too low, in order to minimise the Service Charges, and essential day-to-day maintenance and repair work is regularly ignored, thereby causing inconvenience to owners and decreasing the value of their apartments? Who'll be blamed? The directors.
- What if there's no procedure in place to pursue owners who have Service Charge arrears, and the Management Company runs out of money? Who'll be blamed? The directors.

These sorts of issues exist in many apartment developments in Ireland today, and directors could easily find themselves personally exposed to litigation in relation to these matters.

Powers of directors

To put it simply, the Board of Directors has the power to do whatever is necessary to properly manage the 'business' of the company, subject, of course, to:

- Company law.
- The Memorandum & Articles of Association of the company.
- The terms and provisions of the Lease.

As they act on behalf of the company, they have no authority to do anything that the company itself isn't entitled to do.

Every director must have the best interests of the company in mind when making decisions. They don't have to take any instructions from the other members of the company - ie. the owners. For instance, if the owners want a smaller Sinking Fund - in order to keep their Service Charges lower - it's the legal duty of the directors to consider this issue in the light of the best interests of the Management Company, and not the owners, and then make their decision.

Appointment, removal and rotation of directors

The first directors of the Management Company will be nominated by the developer, and details in relation to these directors must be lodged in a statement with the Registrar of Companies at the same time as the Management Company is formed.

Thereafter, the appointment, removal and rotation of directors is dealt with in the Articles of Association. Most Articles of Association will include the following set of provisions:

- At the first Annual General Meeting of the company, all directors must resign from office.
- At every subsequent AGM, one-third of the directors – those who shall have been longest in office – must resign. If the Board of Directors doesn't consist of three or a multiple of three, the number to resign must be the number nearest one-third.
- If a director dies or resigns, the Articles of Association usually provides that the Board of Directors can temporarily co-opt another director, who must then resign at the next General Meeting of the company.

- Any director who resigns is entitled to offer himself for re-election at that same meeting.
- The members of the company - ie. the owners - have the power to dismiss or remove any director, by ordinary resolution, at a General Meeting of the company. All that's required is a simple majority. The 'weighted' vote - if any - of the original subscribers may be very important in such circumstances - see page 109.

If the developer's subscribers don't have any weighted votes, the time will come very quickly when the voting power of the owners will outweigh that of the subscribers.

This will give the opportunity to the owners to 'take over' the Board of Directors at the first AGM, which must be held no later than eighteen months after the company's formation - see page 116. At the first AGM the existing directors - the developer's nominees - must resign, and this gives the owners the opportunity to elect their own directors onto the Board of Directors.

Taking over the Board of Directors

The following set of circumstances will exist if the owners manage to elect their own representatives onto the Board of Directors before the Management Company Agreement has been completed:

- The management and control of the development will still be under the authority of the developer and his Managing Agent, until such time as he completes the Management Company Agreement under the terms of the Lease. The Management Company, and, therefore, the Board of Directors, has no powers in that regard.
- Although it hasn't any function as yet, the Management Company must comply with company law. Therefore the Board of Directors will have to arrange for the Annual Return to be filed in the Companies Office; the register of members, directors and secretaries to be kept up-to date; the company's books of account to be properly maintained and audited at the end of the financial year - if the company accounts are being used at this stage to manage receipts and payments in the development; and the convening of General Meetings of the company including the AGM - see page 29.
- At this stage, one of the main functions of the Management Company is to join in the signing of the Lease at the sale of any new apartments - see page 8. If the 'owner-directors' refuse or delay the signing of these documents, the develop-

er may not be in a position to sell any more apartments in the development, and that's likely to cause him considerable inconvenience and frustration. The directors may be able to use this situation to negotiate with the developer in relation to aspects of the development with which the owners aren't happy.
- When it comes to the completion of the Management Company Agreement, the directors will be required to sign the Agreement which will transfer the developer's interests and responsibilities to the owners. Although there's a legal duty on the directors to sign this Agreement - the original directors already promised to sign it - they could delay it until they were satisfied that the development was in satisfactory condition, with all major snagging issues completed.

As you can see, there are many consequences in the owners taking over control of the Board of Directors - assuming the voting rights permit them to do so. I'd suggest obtaining legal advice before taking this action, as the new Board of Directors will need assistance from a solicitor if they make this move.

I wouldn't suggest taking this action unless there are serious issues in your development, which the developer or his Managing Agent persistently refuse to address.

Disqualification of directors

There are several circumstances in which a person is automatically disqualified, under company law, from acting as a director:
- Where a person is convicted on indictment of an indictable offence in relation to a company, or an offence involving fraud or deceit.
- Where a person fails to notify the Registrar of Companies that he's disqualified in another State.
- Where a person has been restricted by the courts from acting as a director under Part VII of the Companies Act 1990.
- Where a person is convicted of acting as auditor, liquidator or examiner of a company, while an undischarged bankrupt.
- The Articles of Association can also include other circumstances in which a person can be disqualified from acting as a director of the company.

Should you become a director of the Management Company?

Ordinary members of the company have very little influence over the day-to-day running of the development - that's the responsibility of the Board of Directors. They can, however, increase their influence in the management of the development by amending the Articles of Association but this is a cumbersome enough exercise - see page 122.

If you choose not to become a director of the Management Company, you're choosing a situation for yourself where you've very limited power to influence the day-to-day running and management of your development. If, on the other hand, you become a director, then you and your fellow directors are the individuals legally responsible for the proper management of your development. This responsibility shouldn't be taken lightly.

If you're thinking of putting yourself forward for election as a director you should carefully consider the following:

- Are you prepared to give generously of your time and energy on a voluntary basis to carry out your functions diligently and conscientiously, and inform yourself of all the issues relating to your development?
- Are you prepared to learn about the duties and obligations of company directors under company law?
- Having regard to your lifestyle and working arrangements, will you be in a position to attend most of the meetings of the Board of Directors?
- Are you in fact interested enough in the well-being of your development, and the protection of your investment, to put yourself forward as a director, or are you happy enough to let others make the decisions on your behalf?

If there's no Managing Agent engaged there'll be a considerable amount of work for the directors to handle - negotiations with contractors, supervision of the cleaning and landscaping, the collection of the Service Charges, book-keeping, etc. However, there'll be a lot less day-to-day functions for the directors to carry out if a Managing Agent is engaged.

If you're elected onto the Board of Directors, you'll need to familiarise yourself with important basic information about the Management Company itself, and also any relevant issues concerning your development - see Appendix E.

Directors' meetings

The directors of the Management Company should arrange to meet on a regular basis, to discuss and review all matters relating to the development.

It's important that a directors' meeting is held immediately after the developer has handed over his interests and responsibilities and the first owners' Board of Directors has been elected. A meeting should also be held after each AGM of the company, so that any new directors can familiarise themselves with relevant information regarding the company - see Appendix E.

At that first directors' meeting, the directors should also decide on how often they should meet. This will depend on:

- The nature and size of the development.
- If there's a Managing Agent engaged, and the degree of satisfaction with him.
- The age of the development.

Under company law, minutes of these meetings must be taken and kept with the other official company books, usually at the registered offices of the company. The Director of Corporate Enforcement and company members are entitled to inspect the minutes.

Register of directors and secretaries

A register of directors and secretaries must be kept at the registered office of the company, and it must include the following:

- Each director's name.
- Address.
- Date of birth.
- Nationality.
- Occupation.
- Details of any other directorships held by him.

This register is available for inspection by any member of the public.

Company secretary

The other statutory officer of the Management Company, the company secretary, has clearly defined responsibilities:

- To ensure that the company complies with company law.
- To ensure that the company stays within the provisions of its Memorandum & Articles of Association.

The company secretary acts under the instructions of the Board of Directors. He may also be one of the directors, but this doesn't have to be the case.

The day-to-day functions of the company secretary in a typical apartment development are to:

- Issue new membership or share certificates when an apartment is sold.
- Keep the various company registers up-to-date.
- Ensure that AGM's and EGM's are held in accordance with the Articles of Association, and company law.
- Ensure that the Annual Return is lodged in time in the Companies Office.

The company secretary is a very important officer in any apartment development. If he's negligent in his duties, it can result in the company being struck off the Register of Companies in the Companies Office and heavy fines being imposed on the company.

The company secretary is under the same duty as any director - to act in a competent and diligent manner, and not in a negligent or reckless fashion. He's also subject to the same criminal and civil sanctions and penalties as directors – see page 112.

In the case of Management Companies, the company auditor or Managing Agent is often appointed as company secretary. It's the legal responsibility of the Board of Directors, when appointing a company secretary, to satisfy itself that the person or entity being appointed has the necessary knowledge and experience to properly undertake the functions of company secretary.

In my opinion, I don't think it's a good idea to allow the Managing Agent to act as company secretary, unless the Board of Directors is very satisfied with its relationship with him. I'm aware of cases where Managing Agents have refused to hand over important company documents, including books of account, to the Board of Directors.

A Managing Agent isn't entitled under any circumstances to deny the the Board of Directors access to any of the company documents or records. Under company law, these documents and books are the property of the company.

General Meetings of the Management Company

The owners, as members of the Management Company, exercise control over the company at its General Meetings.

The General Meetings of a company fall into two categories:
- Annual General Meetings (AGM).
- Extraordinary General Meetings (EGM).

The Management Company must hold an AGM every calendar year, and a period of not more than fifteen months can elapse between AGM's.

The first AGM of the company must take place no later than eighteen months after the date of incorporation of the company. In practice this frequently doesn't happen in the case of Management Companies, particularly where the developer hasn't transferred his interests and responsibilities to the owners. Under those circumstances, he still has control of the Management Company, because his original nominees are still the directors of the company.

If the Management Company has failed to hold its first AGM within the eighteen month period, you should contact the Director of Corporate Enforcement, who can compel the directors to hold an AGM.

The directors can arrange to hold the meeting at any time and in any place they wish, provided it's somewhere within the State.

Voting at General Meetings with Service Charge arrears

The voting rights of the members of the Management Company are discussed at page 108 above.

The Articles of Association of your Management Company will contain the provision that you're not entitled to vote at any General Meeting of the Management Company if your Service Charges are in arrears.

Annual General Meeting (AGM)

The AGM of a company is a meeting which must be held in accordance with company law. The Agenda usually follows a particular formula, and deals with the following matters:

- The company's profit and loss account and balance sheet. If the company is limited by guarantee, there'll also be a cash flow statement.
- The directors' report.
- The auditor's report, unless the company is audit exempt.
- The election of directors in place of those retiring.
- The appointment and remuneration of the auditor, unless the company is audit exempt.
- Any other business.

The 'any other business' section is the part of the meeting where members - ie. owners - get the opportunity to discuss any issue relevant to the Management Company, or the apartment development. No decisions can be taken or resolutions put to a vote unless all members entitled to vote have been given due notice of the resolutions.

If you've any motion or resolution which you wish to introduce under 'any other business', you should inform the company secretary who must then include details of the resolution with the notice convening the AGM. A formal vote can then be taken on your motion.

Extraordinary General Meeting (EGM)

An EGM is any General Meeting of the company other than the AGM. An EGM is convened to deal with one or more specific issues. The notice convening the meeting must clearly set out the resolutions to be discussed, and no other issues can be dealt with at the meeting.

Who can call an EGM?

The Board of Directors can call an EGM.

Members of the company can also demand that an EGM be convened. Under Section 132 of the Companies Act 1963, the members themselves can compel the Board of Directors to convene an EGM, provided that the number of members who request such a meeting - 'the requisitionists' - make up at least 10% of the total voting rights of all the members of the company. This is one area where the subscribers weighted voting rights could become an issue - see page 109.

The Board of Directors must, within twenty-one days of receiving such a request, make arrangements for the holding of the EGM, which itself must be held within two months of that date. If the directors fail, neglect or refuse to call the meeting, a number of the requisitionists - representing at least 50% of the voting rights of all the requisitionists - can convene the meeting themselves.

Most of the procedures and issues concerning General Meetings of your Management Company will be found in the Articles of Association of the company

Amending the Articles of Association

The Articles of Association of your Management Company dictate how the company is to conduct its business, and how the Board of Directors is to exercise its powers.

The directors must exercise their powers under the provisions of company law, the Lease and the Articles of Association. In other words, the Board of Directors must keep to a set of rules when making its decisions.

If you want to have more influence in the way the development is

managed, you can seek to have the Articles of Association amended accordingly. There are some instances already discussed in this book where this may be relevant:
- You can include a provision to state the format in which Service Charge invoices and budget details are to be furnished to the owners.
- You can influence the appointment or dismissal of the Managing Agent, by including suitable provisions.
- You can remove the weighted voting rights of the original subscribers nominated by the developer - provided they don't use their weighted votes to defeat the resolution.

The directors must work within those new provisions and all other provisions of the Articles of Association.

You must be careful not to usurp the authority of the Board of Directors, and you should seek legal advice if you wish to amend the Articles of Association, to ensure that there are no long-term detrimental consequences inadvertently hidden in any proposed amendment.

A Special Resolution is needed to amend the Memorandum & Articles of Association. This requires a 75% majority of those present and eligible to vote, in order to be passed.

A Special Resolution can be brought to an EGM, or can be dealt with under 'any other business' at an AGM.

Filing of documents

The Management Company is obliged by law to make an Annual Return to the Companies Office, and this should be done as soon as possible after the AGM.

This Annual Return is normally prepared and filed by the company secretary or auditor. It's a very important responsibility, and the Board of Directors must ensure that it appoints a competent person or body to carry out this function, and also ensure that it's carried out properly.

If the Annual Return isn't filed in time and in the appropriate manner, the Management Company will be liable to prosecution and heavy fines, and will be struck off the Register of Companies in due course.

The purpose of the Annual Return is to provide information about the company to the general public, investors or creditors. Attached to the Annual Return will be certain accounts information. The information required will vary, depending on the type of limited company.

This is another example where I believe that the legal structure of the limited liability company isn't the appropriate vehicle to use for apartment Management Companies.

The costs to the owners of providing the information required under company law - accounting, auditing and legal - are substantial, but the information is of very little use to owners or potential buyers. The Annual Return, under company law, doesn't have to include the type of information which would be of particular interest to existing owners, or potential purchasers in the development, such as:

- The Service Charges.
- The extent of Service Charge arrears.
- The annual budget.
- The Sinking Fund.
- Details of the Managing Agent.
- Any major expenditure pending in the near future.
- Insurance claims over the past twelve months.

Strike-off

Your Management Company could be struck off the Register of Companies for a number of reasons. Among them are:

- Where it fails to file the Annual Return in the Companies Office.
- Where it doesn't have at least two directors.
- Where it doesn't have at least one director living in the Republic of Ireland.

This is an extremely serious situation, and should never be allowed to happen. If this ever does occur to your Management Company, it's hard to see how the directors and company secretary couldn't be held liable.

The consequences of strike-off can be far-reaching:

- All the assets of the Management Company are vested in the Minister for Finance.
- It'll be almost impossible to sell your apartment while the company is in 'strike-off' condition.
- It'll indicate to any potential purchaser that the development is being managed in an extremely unprofessional and careless manner, and would discourage anybody from buying an apartment there.

Restoration

Where a strike-off occurs by reason of the non-filing of the Annual Return, the Companies Office has the power to restore the company, if everything is rectified within a twelve month period. If that solution isn't an option for some reason, the other alternative is to make an application to the High Court for restoration during the following period of twenty years.

Apart from the expense of the restoration itself, there'll also be considerable fines to be paid by the Management Company. These expenses and fines would have to be funded by the owners, who might then be in a position to sue the Board of Directors and/or company secretary for negligence in their duties.

Liability of directors at strike-off

It's important to remember that the Companies Office will give plenty of warning before strike-off, so there's absolutely no excuse for the Board of Directors not complying with the regulations. It isn't uncommon for Management Companies to be struck off the Register of Companies and, in such circumstances, I believe that the Board of Directors and company secretary could be held liable in their personal capacities for:

- The decrease in value of your apartment due to the mismanagement of the company's affairs.
- Any damages suffered by you due to your inability to sell your apartment
- All of the costs and fines applicable to the strike-off and restoration of the company.

Developer's failure to hand over

Every Lease makes provision for the handing over of the development by the developer to the Management Company - see page 14.

Most Leases stipulate when this should occur, and it's usually within a reasonable time after all the units have been sold. Some Leases are less definite, and state that the development should be handed over when the developer considers it appropriate to do so.

Some developers appear to be reluctant to hand over the development. They hold on to their role as Lessor - and keep their own nominees as directors of the Management Company - for many years after the development has been completed.

The most effective way they do this is they retain ownership of one or more of the units, and leave it unsold. Because all of the units aren't sold, the developer considers that he's under no legal obligation under the Lease to hand the development over to the owners.

There may be ways to address this problem -

Company law (1): This approach will only work where each owner has one vote at General Meetings, and there are no weighted votes in favour of the developer's subscribers - see page 109.

Company law states clearly that the first Annual General Meeting must take place within eighteen months of the incorporation of the company. In almost all Memorandum & Articles of Association, it's also stated that the existing directors must resign at this first Annual General Meeting - although they can put themselves forward for re-election if they so wish.

If the developer doesn't arrange for the holding of the first AGM within eighteen months of the company's incorporation, the owners can make an official complaint to the Director of Corporate Enforcement who can compel the holding of such a meeting.

At that first Annual General Meeting, the directors - the original nominees of the developer - will resign. They'll probably put themselves forward for re-election. The owners can refuse to re-elect the outgoing directors, and can elect directors who have been nominated by themselves.

If this is done, the owners will control the Board of Directors, and the situation could become extremely complex and difficult for the developer, particularly if he's still in the process of selling apartments in the development.

When an apartment is sold, the Lease must be signed by the Lessor, the Lessee and directors of the Management Company. If the owners manage to take over the Management Company as outlined above by electing their own Board of Directors, and if those directors refuse to sign any further Leases, the developer would find it very difficult to sell any additional apartments, which might cause considerable distress and inconvenience to him. In such a case the owners may be able to negotiate an agreed date for the handover, in return for co-operation from the owner-directors in signing the Leases.

Any owners contemplating such a move should seek legal advice on the matter before taking such action.

Even if the owners are successful in taking over the Board of Directors of the Management Company in this way, it doesn't mean that they're now in control of the management of the development. This will still remain in the hands of the developer until such time as he transfers his interests and responsibilities under the terms of the Lease - notwithstanding the fact that he has lost control of the Management Company.

Company law (2): If the apartment block is effectively complete and the developer is refusing to hand over the development because he's holding on to one or more apartments, he'll also hold on to the control of the Board of Directors through the weighted voting rights of the first subscribers - provided they have such rights.

If this is the case, I believe that there's a strong possibility that the developer and his nominee directors could be held to be in breach of company law by the suppression of the owners' minority interests.

Contract law: There may be another method by which the owners can try to force the developer to hand over the development - legal proceedings for breach of contract. If the Lease states that the developer agrees to hand over the development when the last apartment has been sold, and if the developer is refusing to hand over the development because he retains ownership of one or more of the apartments, it could be argued that the developer is in breach of an implied term of the Lease - that he would use all his best endeavours to sell all of the apartments. In my opinion there's every possibility that the owners could be successful in such a legal action.

Health & Safety

Health & Safety issues are becoming increasingly prominent in our everyday lives. They're particularly relevant in apartment developments, where there are large numbers of people - owners and their visitors - using the common areas of the property, and there are employees and contractors working on a regular basis.

The Health & Safety regulations revolve around safety at 'places of work', and in 'non-domestic' environments. Whether or not an apartment development is a 'place of work' and a 'non-domestic' environment is debatable. This will depend on the nature of the development, and the manner and regularity in which the contractors - cleaners and landscapers in particular - are employed. Certainly, if any person is employed on a full-time PAYE basis, the apartment development would be considered a 'place of work' under the regulations. It could also be argued that although each individual apartment might be considered a 'domestic environment', the common areas are not.

Regular contractors - cleaners, landscapers or caretakers - may, under certain circumstances, be considered to be employees, even if they're not directly employed on a PAYE basis.

If a duty of care exists under the Safety, Health & Welfare at Work Act 2005, it rests with the person 'in control' of the place of work - the employer. This could be interpreted as the Managing Agent or the Board of Directors, depending on the circumstances.

The duty of care extends beyond a duty to employees only, and encompasses a duty to ordinary members of the public.

Employers are responsible for:

- Maintaining a safe and healthy place of work.
- Evaluating potential hazards to Health & Safety, and putting appropriate safety measures in place.
- Providing the written safety programme in the form of a Safety Statement.

The directors of the Management Company should either seek the advice of a Health & Safety consultant, or carefully study the documentation available from the Health & Safety Authority, in order to ensure that all Health & Safety issues at the development are properly addressed in accordance with the relevant regulations.

If someone is killed or seriously injured in the common areas of an apartment development, the chances are that investigations will be carried out by the Health & Safety Authority and also the Gardaí - under the Non-Fatal Offences Against the Person Act 1997 - to discover the cause of the accident. It would be a very serious matter if such an investigation concluded that the directors of the Management Company, as employers, were negligent, or non-compliant with the Health & Safety regulations.

Under the 2005 Act directors of Management Companies could find themselves liable to very heavy fines and even imprisonment, if found to be in breach of the Act.

Fire safety

In an extensive report, entitled "Successful Apartment Living Part 2", published by Dublin City Council in October 2007, a detailed general survey was carried out at 193 apartment developments in Dublin. According to the findings of the report, three-quarters of the developments surveyed had inadequate fire safety provisions.

The Board of Directors should ensure that a fire safety survey is conducted at the development by a qualified surveyor, on a regular basis. The directors should also implement any recommendations contained in the surveyor's report.

The topic of fire safety is a highly technical issue and it's outside the scope of this book to go into detail, but it's a very important area of responsibility, and must not be ignored by the Board of Directors.

Letting your apartment

There's a provision in most Leases to the effect that, if you're renting out your apartment for a long period of time - for five years and upwards depending on the Lease - you must arrange for your tenant to be registered as a member of the Management Company. This provision will not affect most owner-landlords, as there are very few long-term tenancies of this type to be found in apartment developments in Ireland.

When you rent out your apartment in the usual way - for the usual six or twelve month period - you don't have to notify your Management Company.

However, as you won't be living in the apartment, you should remember in these circumstances to give the Managing Agent:

- Your personal contact details - phone number and email - and postal address.
- Details of at least two keyholders who, apart from the tenant, have access to your apartment and also know the alarm codes, if any - see page 61.

If you also have a car space, it's usually forbidden to let that space separate to your apartment - see page 68.

Your responsibilities as landlord

As an owner-landlord, you're responsible for the actions and behaviour of your tenants. Any breaches of the Lease by your tenants - the duties and obligations set out in your Lease - will, therefore, be regarded by the Management Company as a breach by you in that regard.

In my opinion, the Managing Agent is entitled to charge you for any outlay or expenses - letters, phone calls, etc. - incurred by him, due to a breach of the Lease by your tenants - see page 91. If there's any damage done in the common areas by your tenants, you'll be liable to reimburse the Management Company for the cost of any repairs, clean-ups, etc. It's up to you to have terms in your rental agreement with the tenants, to the effect that you can recover from them any payments which you have to make in these circumstances. As most of the anti-social behaviour which occurs in apartment developments is caused by tenants, I believe that it would be a good idea for every owner-landlord to display a copy of the House Rules in their rented apartment, with a clear note that the tenants are responsible to adhere to the rules or suffer the consequences. The Managing Agent should be able to supply copies of these House Rules.

Complaint to the Management Company by a tenant

Under Section 187 of the Residential Tenancies Act 2004, if your tenant makes a written complaint to you in relation to something for which the Management Company is responsible, you're obliged to forward the complaint to the Management Company. The Board of Directors is also obliged to reply to you indicating the steps, if any, it has taken to deal with the complaint, and you're obliged to forward the letter to your tenant.

Private 'gated' developments

The main difference in relation to the legal structure between an apartment and a house in a private 'gated' development is that you own your house outright and there's no long-term Lease involved.

As with apartment ownership, you also become a member of the Management Company, which owns and manages the common areas of the development.

Most private 'gated' developments are also structured in the form of a limited liability company and, therefore, the rules and regulations outlined above in relation to the Board of Directors, company secretary, General Meetings, voting rights, company strike-off, etc. are equally as relevant to them, as they are to an apartment development.

The Board of Directors should seek advise as to whether or not the development comes under the definition of a 'place of work' in relation to Health & Safety regulations. This can be done by either engaging the services of a consultant, or studying the literature available from the Health & Safety Authority. If considered a 'place of work' under the regulations, the Board of Directors must put the appropriate procedures, Safety Statements, etc. in place, to satisfy the regulations.

The Board of Directors could also instigate a process for the taking-in-charge of the estate by the Local Authority, under Section 180 of the Planning and Development Act 2000, subject to the approval of the majority of house owners. This is a complex and controversial issue which is under review by government agencies, and would require the advice and assistance of planning advisors and the Management Company's solicitor.

Summary

- ◀ Apartment owners have a long leasehold of their own apartment, and collective ownership of the common areas through their Management Company.
- ◀ Owners in a private 'gated' development have freehold ownership of their house, and collective ownership of the common areas through their Management Company.
- ◀ A limited liability company - the Management Company - is established by the developer to eventually manage the development and act as a landlord to the apartment owners.
- ◀ Every Management Company has a Memorandum and Articles of Association, which outlines the functions of the company and the internal rules of operation.
- ◀ The Board of Directors must carry out its functions under the provisions of the Lease, the Memorandum and Articles of Association and company law.
- ◀ Limited liability companies are strictly regulated by company law, and compliance with the regulations is monitored by the Registrar of Companies and the Director of Corporate Enforcement.
- ◀ The Board of Directors and company secretary of the Management Company are accountable for the operations of the company, and are legally responsible to ensure that it complies with company law.
- ◀ The subscribers to the company - nominated by the developer when the company was formed - often have superior voting right to those of the owners.
- ◀ The developer also nominates the first Board of Directors of the company. They must resign at the first AGM but can be re-elected.
- ◀ The officers of the company - directors and company secretary - can face serious sanctions for negligent or incompetent behaviour.
- ◀ The register of directors and secretaries of the Management Company must be available to any member of the public to inspect.
- ◀ Members have the right to vote at General Meetings (AGM's and EGM's) of the Management Company.
- ◀ The register of members of the Management Company must be available to any member of the public to inspect.

- Members can amend the Articles of Association to give themselves more influence in the management of the development.
- Every Management Company must hold an Annual General Meeting, and the first AGM must take place no later than eighteen months after the date of incorporation of the company.
- Every AGM after the first one must be held in every calendar year, and no more than fifteen months can elapse between meetings.
- The Director of Corporate Enforcement can compel the directors to hold the first AGM, if eighteen months has passed since the incorporation of the company. Depending on the various voting rights, the apartment owners may be able to take control of the Board of Directors of the company.
- An Extraordinary General Meeting of the company can be called either by the directors or a group of owners.
- The Management Company must file an Annual Return, and can be struck off the Register of Companies if it fails to do so.
- There may be legal remedies available under company law or contract law to compel a developer to transfer his interests to the owners.
- The Board of Directors must ensure that the development complies with all Health & Safety regulations.
- The Board of Directors should ensure that regular Fire Safety surveys are carried out by competent surveyors.
- An owner who rents out his apartment must ensure that the tenants are aware of the House Rules, and he's responsible if the tenants are in breach of any of them.
- It's normally forbidden to let a car space in an apartment development separate to the apartment itself, or to live in the apartment and let the car space to someone else.

Chapter 8

Insurance Matters

Insurance is a complicated and specialist subject, and in this chapter I intend to give a broad summary of the insurance considerations for your apartment development.

I've always used the services and advice of insurance brokers in all my insurance dealings, and I suggest that this course of action be taken by Boards of Directors of Management Companies in relation to apartment block insurances, as there can be extensive technicalities involved.

The consequences can be quite serious if your apartment development's insurances aren't handled correctly, so I'm merely outlining here the types of insurances which are available to:

- You - as owner of an apartment.
- The Board of Directors - as managers of your development.

All of the insurance policies mentioned contain terms, conditions, exclusions and excesses. You shouldn't take these for granted. They're very detailed and very important, and should be fully examined and understood. Your insurance broker is the person to advise you in that regard.

Copy of insurance policy

As a member of the Management Company, you're entitled to obtain a copy of the block policy document from the Managing Agent. Your solicitor will have requested a copy of the current policy when you were buying your apartment.

The Managing Agent is entitled to charge a reasonable fee for providing you with a copy of the policy document - you'll find this provision in most Leases.

If you're considering buying a second-hand apartment, you should request from the auctioneer a copy of the insurance claims history for the development in question. This might give you some insight as to how the development is being managed, and might help to highlight any specific issues, such as persistent vandalism.

Duty to insure

It's the duty of the Board of Directors of the Management Company to ensure that there's adequate insurance cover on the development, and this duty will be set out in detail in the Lease.

The Managing Agent often takes over this responsibility, but the Board of Directors must give appropriate and clear instructions to the Managing Agent in relation to property valuations, excesses, etc.

The Board of Directors should regularly monitor the levels of insurance at the development. The matter should be discussed at the first directors' meeting following each AGM, so that incoming directors can familiarise themselves with the details.

Insurance matters are so important that I recommend that all communications between the Board of Directors and the Managing Agent should be in writing, for the protection of both parties, and as a matter of record.

Insurance at startup

The general block insurance policy will initially be arranged by the developer or his Managing Agent. They'll complete the proposal form which establishes the contract with the insurance company.

As soon as the developer transfers his interests and responsibilities to the Management Company, the Board of Directors becomes legally responsible for insurances at your development. It's very important, at that stage, that the insurance cover and property valuations be reviewed by the newly elected Board of Directors in conjunction with the Managing Agent.

Reinstatement valuation

One of the main issues which the Managing Agent must keep under review is the reinstatement valuation of the buildings. This should be reviewed every year.

The reinstatement valuation is the full cost of rebuilding your development - all of the structures and common areas - should it be totally destroyed. The figure must include the cost of removing debris from the site, and the professional fees - architects, engineers, surveyors, etc.

The developer, or his architect, provides this figure for the initial insurance policy, but experience shows that this figure in some instances is inaccurate - ie. too low. It's vitally important, therefore, that the incoming Board of Directors engages an independent surveyor to calculate the reinstatement valuation for insurance purposes as soon as the owners take control of your development. You shouldn't assume that the figure is correct merely because the developer's architect provided it some time ago.

The surveyor will use the architect's plans and drawings to calculate the reinstatement valuation. It's quite a meticulous exercise when carried out for the first time. Any revised valuation figures should be sent to the insurance broker, and the policy will be adjusted accordingly. If the reinstatement valuation is revised upwards, the insurance premium may increase.

The reinstatement valuation should be updated every year and forwarded to the insurance broker before the renewal of the block insurance policy.

The reinstatement valuation date should extend for a period of at least two years *after* the policy's renewal date. In other words, if the policy runs from January to December, it's not sufficient to obtain a reinstatement figure which only extends up to the end of December. Let's take a situation where there's a major claim involving serious damage to an apartment building occurring in, say, November. A reinstatement valuation up to December will be inadequate, as it's likely that the actual demolition or building work won't take place for a considerable period of time - maybe over a year or more - after that date.

The reinstatement valuation becomes a simpler operation after the initial exercise, because, in subsequent years, the surveyor can use his original notes and calculations to arrive at the updated figures, without having to consult the architect's plans.

The directors could be found to be negligent in the conduct of their duties if they fail to instruct the Managing Agent to insure the development for the proper reinstatement valuation. They should also check that this has been done. It's a matter that must be kept under constant review in the management of the development.

Insurance policies required for an apartment development

Block insurance policy

There are several insurance companies offering apartment block insurance in Ireland. The insurance cover extends to all the apartment buildings as well as the common areas.

In general, the liabilities and perils which are covered include damage to any part of the apartment development - including the individual apartments, arising from:

- Fire.
- Stealing, involving entry by forcible or violent means.
- Vandalism.
- Storm or flood.
- Water leaks.
- Damage caused by falling objects - aerials, satellite dishes, etc.
- Domestic fuel oil leaks.
- Falling trees or branches.
- Subsidence.
- Other accidental damage.

Usually there's further additional cover provided in relation to landscaping, fire brigade charges, replacement of locks, etc., and these will all be outlined in the policy document.

Most policies also provide a sum of money payable for alternative accommodation, should any apartment become uninhabitable due to any of the perils insured under the policy. There's usually a limit on the amount of money payable under this section, based on a percentage of the overall sum insured.

Employers' liability insurance

The block insurance policy usually covers the Management Company's liability in relation to any person directly employed in the development, such as a caretaker, concierge, etc.

This doesn't cover the independent contractors - electricians, cleaners, plumbers, etc. - who are contracted from time to time to do a specific job, and who provide their own employees and materials. These outside contractors must have their own insurance cover, and it's very important that the Managing Agent checks that they have sufficient insurance before hiring them - otherwise the Managing Agent may be held liable if damage or injury is caused either by or to these contractors.

Property owners' liability insurance

This cover which also forms part of the block insurance policy provides indemnity for:

- The Management Company - as owner of the freehold of apartment development.
- You - as owner of your own individual apartment within your development.

Property owners' liability insurance relates to any damage or injury caused, or where liability occurs within the development, by virtue of your ownership of the property.

This insurance doesn't cover you for any liabilities you may have to visitors or tenants for accidents or damage occurring within your own apartment. You'll need to take out your own personal liability insurance to cover that risk.

Engineering insurance

If there are engineering installations in the apartment development - lifts, boilers, compressors, etc. - the Board of Directors must take out specific insurance cover known as 'engineering insurance', so that an insurance company can issue statutory inspection certificates on a regular basis for the equipment. This insurance is compulsory in law, and if the Board of Directors fails or neglects to take out such insurance, it's liable to criminal prosecution.

This insurance also covers any damage caused to the equipment, as a result of a breakdown.

Regardless of the engineering insurance policy, all engineering installations should also have annual maintenance contracts as part of the proper management of the development.

Individual insurance cover

All your liabilities, as an owner of an apartment within your development and also as a member of the Management Company, will be covered under the block insurance policy.

However, there are two important areas where you *don't* have any insurance cover under the block insurance policies:

- The contents of your own apartment and your own personal belongings.
- Your liabilities as a property owner *within* your own apartment - liabilities to the occupiers and any visitors to your apartment.

You should take out insurance to cover these liabilities. There are plenty of policies available which will fulfil your requirements, and you should seek the advice of an insurance broker to make sure that you're covered for all eventualities.

A similar situation can occur in relation to tenants in your apartment. They should also have insurance cover for their own belongings, and also liability insurance, as occupier, to cover any accidents or damage caused to their visitors as a result of their own personal negligence. Such liability isn't covered either by the block insurance policy, or by your insurance policy as owner of the apartment.

Directors' & Officers' liability insurance

This is an aspect of apartment management which should be of very great concern to all directors of Management Companies.

Let's take it that you decide to get involved in the management of your apartment development and you agree to become one of the directors of the Management Company.

As a company director you've considerable legal responsibilities. Apart from the fact that you're going to have to devote a considerable amount of your time to carry out your functions properly, you should also be aware that, by becoming a director of the Management Company, you're exposing yourself to personal financial risk.

As a director of the Management Company, you've a duty to carry on the 'business' of the company in a responsible and diligent manner, exercising due care, skill and attention in all matters relating to the company. In other words, you must not be negligent in the exercise of your role as company director - see page 113.

The 'business' of the Management Company, as stated in the Lease and the Memorandum & Articles of Association of the company, is to properly manage and maintain the apartment development. If you're seen to be negligent in carrying out your role as director - particularly in relation to the administration of the company itself - and a complaint is made against you, the matter may come to the notice of the Director of Corporate Enforcement, and he has the authority to institute criminal proceedings against you.

If, due to the actions - or more probably the inactions - of the Board of Directors, an owner suffers inconvenience, distress or financial loss, he's entitled to sue you as a director, in your personal capacity, for damages in the civil courts.

The fact that:
- You took on the office of director with the best will in the world.
- You've no experience.
- You're in receipt of no pay for your labours,

won't be taken into consideration in legal proceedings.

It's for this reason that there's an insurance cover available called 'Directors' & Officers' liability insurance', which will provide you with financial protection against any court proceedings taken against you in your capacity as a director. Every director of a Management Company should ensure that there's a Directors' & Officers' liability insurance policy taken out on his behalf.

The cost of the premium will form part of the annual budget, and will be incorporated in the Service Charges, which all owners pay.

Without the protection of Directors' & Officers' liability insurance, directors are leaving themselves personally exposed to litigation if something goes wrong.

Premium payment plans

The insurance premiums usually represent one of the highest cost factors in the annual budget, and can seriously affect the Management Company's cash flow – particularly if the premiums have to be paid early in the financial year when many of the Service Charges haven't been collected.

The way to combat this cash flow problem is to opt for a 'premium payment plan', whereby the premium is paid off monthly over a period of ten months. There's a relatively modest charge for this facility – usually about 4% - and it's a very good way of alleviating any potential cash flow problems in the Management Company's accounts.

The insurance broker will have all the details.

Policy excesses

Most insurance policies have an 'excess clause', whereby the insured person must bear a certain initial cost in relation to each claim. This can vary depending on the insurance company providing the policy, and some insurance companies offer a selection of excess levels.

The insurance premium is usually lowered if a higher excess is chosen.

Undoubtedly, your block insurance policy will have an excess clause. However, as there'll be many different opinions on the matter, it would be the prudent Board of Directors that leaves the decision as to the amount of the excess to the owners, at a General Meeting of the company or an informal pre-budget meeting.

At this meeting, the owners should also decide on who should cover the expense of the excess on the policy. Should the owner have to bear the cost of this excess or should the Management Company pay the excess to the owner in the event of a claim? If a decision is made on this question, it'll alleviate disputes and arguments later.

These are decisions that can be delegated by the Board of Directors to the owners, as they don't affect the 'business' of the company - the proper management of the development.

Removal from insurance policy

The provision of adequate insurance cover is one of the services which the Board of Directors must provide for you, under the terms of your Lease. Another service that the Management Company agrees to provide for you under the Lease is to note your name and the name of your lending institution, as interested parties, on the insurance policy.

However, it's also stated elsewhere in your Lease, that the Board of Directors isn't obliged to provide you with any services whatsoever, if you're in breach of the terms of your Lease, or don't pay your Service Charge.

It *may be* within the rights of the Board of Directors to remove your name and that of your lending institution, as interested parties, from the insurance policy if you don't pay your Service Charge, and are therefore in breach of the terms of your Lease.

This is a serious matter, and is dealt with in detail at page 92.

Private 'gated' developments

In most private 'gated' developments, each house owner arranges and pays for his own household insurance with his own preferred insurance broker or insurance company.

The Management Company arranges the insurances for the common areas, and all owners contribute towards this premium through their Service Charges. The main insurance consideration is for public liability and, perhaps, employers' liability insurance, although in some cases engineering insurance and the insurance of certain plant and machinery may also be involved.

It's still an important matter for the Board of Directors in a private 'gated' development to consider taking out Directors' & Officers' liability insurance, for all the reasons outlined above.

Summary

- All Management Companies should engage the services of a professional insurance broker to look after the insurance needs of the development.
- Each owner is entitled to a copy of the block insurance policy. The Management Company is entitled to charge a fee for providing it.
- The Board of Directors of the Management Company is under strict liability to ensure that there's adequate insurance cover for the development.
- Initial insurance cover is arranged by the developer, and the details should be checked by the new Board of Directors when he transfers his interests and responsibilities to the owners.
- The block insurance policy usually includes employers' liability insurance and property owners' liability insurance.
- An engineering insurance policy might also be required by law.
- A reinstatement valuation should be carried out every year.
- The block insurance policy doesn't cover the contents of each individual owner's apartment, or his legal liabilities within the walls of his apartment, and separate insurance should be taken out by each individual owner to cover this.
- Tenants should also have an insurance policy to cover their own contents and liabilities.
- Every Board of Directors should arrange Directors' & Officers' liability insurance to cover the directors' exposure to litigation.
- In private 'gated' developments, each house owner usually insures his own house, and contributes to the collective liability insurances for the common areas.

Appendix A

Glossary of Terms
(and their use in this book)

Annual General Meeting (AGM)
This is one of the official General Meetings of the Management Company. It must be held every year under company law. The term is regularly shortened to 'AGM'. There's a standard Agenda specific to Annual General Meetings, and the AGM must conclude certain business under company law. There's also an 'any other business' section, which allows the owners to discuss any matters they wish - see page 121.

Annual Return
This is a document which must be filed every year in the Companies Office. It contains certain information about the Management Company. The Annual Return is available to any member of the public to examine. Heavy penalties are imposed on the Management Company, and the Board of Directors, if the Annual Return isn't filed in accordance with company law - see page 123.

Block insurance policy
This is the main insurance policy for the apartment development. It usually includes property damage cover, property owners' liability cover and employers' liability cover - see page 135.

Board of Directors
In this book, the Board of Directors will always mean the Board of Directors of the Management Company. It controls the 'business' of the company, and carries the responsibility to ensure that the duties and obligations of the Management Company are fulfilled in accordance with the terms of the Lease, the Articles of Association and company law. The Board of Directors is referred to in some Leases as the Management Committee or the Governing Committee.

When the Management Company is first incorporated, the Board of Directors consists of nominees of the developer. These first directors probably won't own any apartments in the development. When the developer transfers his interests and responsibilities to the owners, they'll elect their own Board of Directors, which will then control the management of the development - see page 110.

Common areas
These are the areas of the development which are not owned by any individual, and are under the direct control of the Board of Directors of the Management Company. They mainly consist of the grounds of the development, stairwells and corridors, lifts, bin stores, bike sheds and the car park - see page 25.

Company secretary
This is an officer of the Management Company - who may or may not be a director - who is responsible to ensure that the administrative, legal and financial workings of the company are in compliance with company law. The company secretary officially calls the General Meetings of the company, and has the responsibility to ensure that the Annual Return is filed in the Companies Office. Anybody is legally entitled to act as company secretary, but in most cases it's either the Managing Agent or the company auditor who is appointed - see page 119.

Covenants
This is the legal term in the apartment Lease for the promises or pledges made by the various parties to the Lease. Covenants of the Lessor are the promises made by the developer, and covenants of the Lessee are the promises made by the apartment owner. The Management Company also enters into a covenant in the Lease to take over the duties and responsibilities of the developer when he transfers his interests to it - see pages 8, 27 and 42.

Developer
This is the person or company who has built the apartment development and has sold the apartments. He's also referred to in this book - and in the apartment Lease - as the Lessor, as he's the person who gives the buyers the Lease on their apartments. He's in the position of landlord until he transfers his interests and responsibilities in the development to the owners - see page 14.

Easements
This is the legal term in the Lease for various additional rights which attach to the ownership of an apartment. It usually refers to the right-of-way over the common areas for the apartment owners and their visitors, and also the pipes and cables which connect to each individual apartment - see page 24.

Estate
In the Lease, the Estate normally refers to the land and property

which makes up the apartment development - the common areas and all of the apartments.

Extraordinary General Meeting (EGM)

This term refers to every official General Meeting of the Management Company, other than the Annual General Meeting. The term is regularly shortened to 'EGM'. An EGM is usually called to discuss a specific issue, and can be called - through the company secretary - by either the Board of Directors, or by a number of owners - see page 122.

Freehold

This is a form of absolute legal ownership of property where there's no lease for a term of years, and the property never has to be handed back to anybody at any time - see page 2.

General Meetings of the company

A General Meeting of the company is the official name for either the Annual General Meeting (AGM), or any Extraordinary General Meeting (EGM) of the Management Company. Any such meeting must be conducted in accordance with company law and the Articles of Association of the company. Other meetings of apartment owners can be held on an informal basis to discuss certain issues, such as insurance matters or the annual budget, but they won't be considered official meetings of the company, and therefore no legally binding resolutions or motions can be passed - see page 120.

Governing committee

This term is used in some Leases to refer to the Board of Directors of the Management Company.

House Rules

The House Rules is the set of duties and obligations which pertain to the behaviour of occupiers - owners or tenants - in the development. A comprehensive list will be contained in each Lease.

Lease

The Lease - with a capital 'L' in this book - is the Lease of the apartment by the owner, and is the cornerstone of your Title Documents to your apartment. It contains among other things the duties and obligations of the apartment owners and the Management Company, together with details of Service Charge calculations, etc. Most Leases are for a very long period of time, stretching into many hundreds of years.

You should insist on receiving a copy of your Lease at sale closing.

Leasehold

This is the legal form of ownership which every apartment owner has over his apartment. It's a class of limited ownership, whereby the 'owner' has the use and enjoyment of the property for a specific period of time, after which he must return it to the Lessor. In the case of apartment developments, the apartment is returned to the Management Company. The leasehold interest term-of-years in most apartments is so long that it's often referred to as a 'quasi-freehold' or 'virtual freehold' interest - see page 2.

Lessee

The Lessee - with a capital 'L' in this book - is the person who has bought an apartment and to whom the Lease is given - the apartment owner - see page 7.

Lessor

The Lessor - with a capital 'L' in this book - is the person who gives the Lease and who holds the freehold interest in the apartment. The developer is the original Lessor. When the developer transfers his interests and responsibilities to the Management Company, it takes over the role of Lessor and holds the freehold of the apartments, along with the common areas - see page 7.

Management Committee

This term is used in some Leases to refer to the Board of Directors of the Management Company.

Management Company Agreement

This is the Agreement which the developer enters into with the Management Company before any of the apartments are sold, in which he agrees to hand over his interests and responsibilities in your apartment development to the Management Company. He promises to do this at an unspecified date in the future - usually when all of the apartments have been sold - and for a nominal sum.

In this Agreement, the Management Company also agrees to accept the interests and obligations of the developer at the appropriate completion date.

There'll be a reference to this Management Company Agreement in your Lease - see page 8.

Management Company

The term 'Management Company' is often confused by owners with the term 'Managing Agent'. They are two entirely different entities.

The Management Company is the limited liability company which was formed by the developer at the start of your development. It's the body which will own the freehold of the entire apartment development, and will be responsible for the management and control of the development - once the developer transfers his interests and responsibilities to it. It's like a sophisticated 'Owners' Association'.

Whenever the term 'Management Company' is used in this book *in relation to the management of the apartment development* it should be read as:

- 'the developer' in developments where the developer hasn't yet transferred his interests and responsibilities to the Management Company. Until such time as this happens, the Management Company has no role or function in the management of the development.
- 'The Board of Directors', if the development has been transferred by the developer to the owners. He does this by transferring it to the Management Company.

You become a member of the Management Company when you buy your apartment, and you control the company through the General Meetings of the company. It's *your* Management Company.

When the term of years in your Lease expires, you must surrender your apartment back to your Management Company.

Managing Agent

The term 'Managing Agent' is often confused by owners with the term 'Management Company'.

In most apartment developments, the directors of the Management Company don't wish to personally carry out the management functions which are their responsibility to perform - such as, hire the various cleaning and landscaping contractors, manage the domestic waste, collect the Service Charges, manage the accounts, etc.

They therefore engage an independent contractor who specialises in this type of property management, and this contractor acts as an agent to the Board of Directors - hence the term 'Managing Agent'.

At the initial stages of an apartment development, the developer, who likewise doesn't want to become directly involved in the management of the development, will engage a firm of property managers to act as the Managing Agent. The Managing Agent only acts for the developer in relation to *the management of the development under the terms of the Lease*. He has no function or authority in relation to the building, design or snagging of the development.

In this book you must replace the term 'Managing Agent' with the term 'Board of Directors' for any development where the developer, or the Management Company directors, are not engaging the services of a Managing Agent, but are managing the development on a day-to-day basis themselves - see page 31.

Member of the company

You become a member of the Management Company when you buy your apartment. This means that you're a stakeholder in the company.

You control the company through the General Meetings of the company. You don't control the management of your development - this is done by the Board of Directors of the Management Company.

The main influence you have in the actual management of your development is to 'hire and fire' the directors, and to make amendments to the Articles of Association of the company - see page 107.

Memorandum & Articles of Association of the company

This is a document which sets out the 'business' of the Management Company, and outlines the rules and procedures under which the company is to operate. A copy of this document can be obtained in relation to any company from the Companies Office or through their website - see page 106 and Appendix H.

Officer of the company

This is a legal term and refers to either a director of the company, or the company secretary.

Owner-occupier

This description is used in the book for a person who has bought an apartment and is living in it.

Owner-landlord

This description is used in the book for a person who has bought an apartment as an investment, and is renting it out to tenants.

Premises

This is the term used in most Leases to describe the entirety of the property in the possession of an owner - whether by lease or licence - and will consist of the apartment, together with car space and balcony, if any.

Private 'gated' development

A private 'gated' development is a development consisting of private houses and perhaps some apartments. The difference between such a development and a regular suburban housing estate is that, even if it only consists of private houses, a private 'gated' development is developed with the understanding that the common grounds would not be taken in charge by the Local Authority, but would be owned and managed by a Management Company, in the same way as the common areas of an apartment development.

Whether or not there are gates at the entrance is irrelevant, but in most cases there are gates through which only the occupiers have access.

Many of these developments have been intentionally designed in this fashion by the developer. In other cases, it was part of the Planning Permission conditions that the estate wouldn't be taken in charge by the Local Authorities, but would be managed by a Management Company.

Requisitions on Title

This is a set of specific questions which are prepared by the solicitor for the buyer of a property - new and second-hand - and forwarded to the solicitor for the seller. The Requisitions on Title form seeks information on a variety of matters such as proper title to the land, details on the legal status of the Management Company, Service Charge arrears on the apartment in question, insurance policies, and a host of other details.

No buyer of a property should ever complete the purchase unless satisfactory replies to the Requisitions on Title have been received and examined by their solicitor - see page 18.

Reserved property

Also known as 'retained lands'. This legal term will be found in most Leases, and refers to those parts of the development which are in the ownership and control of the Management Company, but which don't fall into the category of common areas. Your car space and balcony usually form part of the reserved property. You've exclusive use of those places so they don't form part of the common area, but the Management Company owns and is responsible for them.

Reversionary interest

If a person owns a property and leases it out to another person, he can't enjoy the benefits of the property during the period of the lease - he has guaranteed the lessee 'quiet enjoyment' of the property throughout the period of the lease. Although, in most cases, he still owns a freehold interest in the property he doesn't enjoy possession of the property until the period of the lease has expired and the property *reverts* back to him. He, therefore, has a reversionary interest in the property.

The developer, at first, owns the reversionary interest in each apartment and the Management Company will eventually own it when the developer transfers his interests and responsibilities to the Management Company. The owner enjoys the benefits and possession of the apartment throughout the period of the Lease, but the apartment ultimately reverts back to the ownership of the Management Company when the period of the apartment Lease expires.

Service Charge

This is the annual sum of money which is levied on each apartment owner, to cover the annual cost of managing the apartment development and administering the Management Company. It's calculated as a percentage of the annual budget, and the method of calculation will be clearly expressed in each apartment Lease - see page 73.

Sinking Fund

This is also known as a Reserve Fund in some Leases.

A contribution to the Sinking Fund is one of the cost headings in the annual budget, and the purpose of creating the fund is to build up a sum of money over a period of time which will cover future major expenditures within the development.

Every apartment Lease makes specific provision for a Sinking Fund. The Board of Directors of the Management Company has a legal duty to establish and maintain an adequate Sinking Fund - see page 83.

Subscriber

The subscribers to the Memorandum & Articles of Association of the Company are the first members of the Management Company, and are nominated by the developer, when he incorporates the Management Company as a limited liability company at the start of a new apartment development - see pages 5 and 14.

Although it's unlikely that they'll own any apartments in the development, they have voting rights at General Meetings of the company. Sometimes they have voting rights far above those of the owners themselves - see page 109.

Tenant

In this book, the term is used for any person who is renting an apartment from an owner-landlord.

APPENDIX B

Checklist before you buy an apartment

Much of the information which you require before buying an apartment is quite different to that which you require when buying a regular house in a suburban housing estate.

Many of the items below won't be relevant if you're buying a new apartment in a new development, and those particular items will be fairly obvious.

Regardless of what you intend to buy, your solicitor and lending institution will insist that a proper survey is carried out by a qualified surveyor to ascertain the value of the property in question.

I'll assume that you'll check out the physical condition of the apartment itself - interior of the apartment and exterior of the building including common areas - to satisfy yourself that it suits your needs and that it's worth the asking price.

However, because of the particular nature of apartment living there are other concerns which your solicitor, or you, should check in order to be satisfied about what you're buying.

Few potential buyers seek the kind of comprehensive information about the apartment development, the management structure or management accounts, which they really need in order to be fully informed. I can only speculate as to the reasons for this:

- They're not aware of what they're buying into when they buy an apartment, and therefore don't know what to look for.
- They assume that the auctioneer will provide them with all of the relevant information which they require.
- They assume that their solicitor has made all of the relevant enquiries on their behalf. Solicitors normally send a formal document to the seller's solicitor requesting certain information. This form is known as a 'Requisitions on Title' and is in a standard format approved by the Law Society of Ireland. This form requests specific information about the development and the Management Company. It's a comprehensive check-list from a legal perspective, and the replies to the questions give some indications as to the state of management of the apartment development. Replies to the Requisitions on Title should be obtained before the Contract of Sale is signed by the buyer, but this isn't always possible.

Being realistic about this exercise I'd have to say that you'll probably find it difficult, or impossible, to obtain some of the information which you seek, for various reasons:

- Neither the seller's solicitor nor the auctioneer will have all of the information you want. A lot of the information sought on the check-list below would need to be furnished by the Managing Agent. As some of the information isn't in the public domain, the Managing Agent would need the permission of the Board of Directors of the Management Company, in order to provide you with the details which you seek - eg. insurance claims history, reinstatement valuations, etc.
- If there isn't a Managing Agent engaged by the Board of Directors, and the directors are managing the development themselves, there probably isn't any person designated to provide this information.
- There are no legal systems in place to have this information readily available. In many instances, it may not be available due to poor record-keeping by the Managing Agent.
- The Managing Agent isn't legally bound to provide you with this information.
- The Board of Directors may not wish to allow private information about the development to be given to you, even though you're a potential new member of the Management Company.

Checklist

1. How many apartments are in the development? Developments with a small number of units tend to have proportionately higher Service Charges, because all the administration costs and professional fees are being shared by a smaller number of owners.

2. If there's a number of apartment buildings in the development, are they under separate management structures, or is there one collective management structure for the entire development? If there are separate management structures for each block, this again will contribute to greater administration costs and consequently higher Service Charges. If this is the case, what are the arrangements for the collective management of the common areas?

3. Are you satisfied with the state of cleanliness and repair of the internal common areas of your block, and the external landscaped areas, car park, etc.? Remember that the larger and more elaborate the features are, the greater the cost of maintaining them. Sophisti-

cated water features may look great, but they can be expensive to maintain and insure. You shouldn't be influenced too much by the sales brochure for a new development. The developer is under no legal obligation to you to complete the development as per the brochure. His only obligation to you is to complete your specific apartment as per the specifications, and to complete the overall development as per the Planning Permission. You'll find that this is clearly set out in your Lease. If you wish to know exactly what facilities should be included in the common areas, you must check the actual Planning Permission granted by the Local Authority, together with the accompanying plans and drawings. As a member of the public, you're entitled to view these documents.

4. Are there bicycles locked to railings, or in other unauthorised locations in the common areas? If so, it's an indication that the House Rules are not being enforced.

5. You should visit the development at night to check out the common area lighting. Is the lighting adequate, and are all the lights working properly?

6. Examine all the entrances into the development, in particular any automatic gates and doors. Are there swipe-cards, keys or codes used? Do you feel that the arrangements provide sufficient security?

7. Are the lifts in your apartment building operating properly?

8. Where's your apartment located in relation to any gates or entrance doors, lifts or water pumps at the development? The constant opening and closing of security gates and doors can be noisy and annoying to owners of apartments located near them, as also are lifts and water pumps.

9. Are you happy with the overall security within the development, taking into consideration its location? Are there CCTV cameras installed? Are they false cameras, or do they really work? A working CCTV system can be very expensive to maintain. Developers tend to have little regard for security in the course of designing and building apartments. It's usually left up to the owners to take additional security measures if required, when the development has been completed.

10. What are the conditions of the bin store and bike shed? These two areas are good indicators as to the proper management of the development, as they tend to get cluttered and dirty very quickly if not properly maintained and monitored.

11. Are copies of the House Rules clearly displayed in the common

areas, together with contact details for the Managing Agent, and emergency contact numbers?

12. Are you happy with the other signage throughout the development - apartment numbers, directional signs, fire exits, general management signs?

13. Details in relation to the Sinking Fund will be sought in your solicitor's Requisitions on Title. You should pay particular attention to this when buying in an older development. You should satisfy yourself that there's a sufficient Sinking Fund available to cover large expenditures in relation to refurbishment works, lift replacement, etc., which may become due in the near future.

14. If you're allocated a parking space, is it properly marked out, and is it large enough for you to park your car? Or is the car park a 'free-for-all'? What are the parking arrangements for your visitors? Car parking can be an extremely contentious and frustrating issue among occupiers, so you need to be absolutely clear that the parking arrangements will suit you.

15. Are there any professional surveys available in relation to the development - reinstatement valuations, Health & Safety surveys, Fire surveys? If any of these surveys exist - and in many cases they won't - you should try to get copies of them and check that any recommendations contained in them have been addressed. Such surveys are unlikely to exist in the case of new developments not yet fully occupied - it would be up to the owners to commission any such reports when they take control.

16. Is there a Safety Statement available for the development, and is it displayed?

17. What is the official name of the Management Company? Check the details in the Companies Office or on their website. Any member of the public is entitled to obtain this information - in some cases you have to pay a small fee to obtain copies of documents. The information available includes:

- The registered offices of the company.
- The date it was incorporated.
- The last filing date of the Annual Return.
- Copies of any Annual Returns filed.
- The names and addresses of directors, company secretary, auditor, etc.
- Certain accounts information depending on the type of company.

- The Memorandum & Articles of Association of the company.

18. Ask for accounts information from the Managing Agent. Check out the situation in relation to debtors in particular, as this will give you an indication as to the extent of Service Charge arrears. If there are considerable amounts of arrears, it'll indicate to you, that:
- There are inadequate procedures in place for pursuing Service Charge arrears.
- There are problems with the development which have resulted in owners withholding their Service Charges.

19. Has the developer handed over the development? If not, has he developed any other apartment developments, and has he handed them over to the various Management Companies?

20. When was the Management Company incorporated? If it's longer than eighteen months ago, has the first Annual General Meeting been held?

21. Check out a copy of the Lease. The Managing Agent will have a copy. There's quite a lot of legal jargon in this document, as it represents the main Title Document for your apartment, but there's also a lot of important information. Your solicitor should discuss this with you in detail. Before you make your decision to buy, you should check out the duties and obligations of all parties - the Lessor (developer), the Lessee (owner) and the Management Company. How are the Service Charges apportioned between the apartments? Can interest be levied on overdue Service Charges? Is it forbidden to fit wooden floors in the apartment - and is that important to you?

22. Check out the Articles of Association of the Management Company and, in particular, the voting rights of the members. If the developer hasn't yet handed over the development, do the first subscribers to the company have weighted voting rights?

23. Is there a Managing Agent? What's his name? This information should be available from the auctioneer. Who appointed the Managing Agent, and is there a written contract in place? If the development hasn't been handed over by the developer, the chances are that the Managing Agent is his appointee. For how long has the Managing Agent been appointed, and how can the contract be terminated? What's the Managing Agent's fee? Does he have professional indemnity insurance and bonding?

24. Find out the amount of the Service Charge on the apartment. If it's a second-hand apartment, check out the Service Charge amounts over the previous few years, and if there are any projected Service Charge figures for future years. If it's a new apartment,

keep in mind that the first year's Service Charge is usually artificially low to induce people to buy the apartments. Ask to see the budget on which the Service Charge was calculated.

25. Who controls the account where the Service Charges are lodged?

26. What's the breakdown of owner-occupiers and owner-landlords in the development? This information may not be available, but the Managing Agent may be able to give you an estimate of the percentage of apartments in the development which are rented out to tenants. Ask the company secretary to show you the register of members, which will give you the names and addresses of all the owners - you're legally entitled to see this register - see page 108.

27. Ask the company secretary to show you the register of directors and secretaries - see page 119.

28. Check in the Companies Office to see if any Extraordinary General Meetings of the Management Company have been held, and check the resolutions passed.

29. What's the insurance claims history in the development? This information should be available from the insurance broker or Managing Agent. If there have been several claims for damage or breakage, it might suggest that there's a problem with vandalism and security in the development.

30. Are there any public rights-of-way through the development? This could have an affect on the levels of security and maintenance required, and could also influence the insurance premiums in relation to public liability.

31. If you've decided to buy the apartment and have paid a deposit, your solicitor will request formal replies to Requisitions on Title. There'll be a considerable amount of additional relevant information contained in that document. Tell your solicitor that you want to see a copy of the replies to Requisitions on Title, if possible before you sign the Contract of Sale.

Private 'gated' development

Some of the above details are obviously not required to be checked if you're thinking of buying a house in a private gated development but most of the points are relevant.

However, as with apartment developments, be prepared to be frustrated when you discover that some of the information will not be forthcoming, or simply won't be available.

APPENDIX C

Checklist before appointing a Managing Agent

This Appendix should be read in conjunction with Appendix D, where you can see the extent of the services which are available from most Managing Agents.

1. What is the management fee proposed to be charged? Does the fee include VAT? What services are included in the fee, and what services are *not* included in the fee?

2. Do you collect your fee in a single payment at the beginning of the year, in monthly instalments, or in a single payment at the end of the year?

3. Do you have professional indemnity insurance? What is your level of cover? Can we see the documents?

4. Do you have financial bonding and to what amount? Can we see the documents?

5. Are you registered under the Data Protection Act?

6. How many years have you been in the Managing Agent business?

7. List the multi-unit developments which you currently manage and the number of units in each.

8. List all the staff who will be dealing with our development, and their qualifications and experience.

9. In addition to the management fee, are there any instances where you also charge a percentage of any contractors' fees or insurance premiums? See page 84

10. Are all of your contractors independent of your company, or does any employee or director of your company have any interest - financial or otherwise - in any of the contractors you intend to use in our development?

11. How often are routine inspection visits to our development carried out by your company? Are these visits included in the management fee? What do you propose to charge for non-scheduled visits to our development?

12. How do you propose to deal with the Management Company's bank accounts including the Sinking Fund?

13. Furnish samples of the financial and budget information which

will be provided to owners with their annual Service Charge invoice.

14. Can you provide company secretarial services, and what is your fee for this service?

15. How do you propose to deal with the collection of Service Charges and, in particular, any Service Charge arrears?

16. How do you propose to deal with breaches of the Lease by the owners and occupiers?

17. What facilities do you have at your offices to maintain all the records of the Management Company - accounts, membership and incidents?

18. How is the financial information prepared and provided to the Management Company's auditors?

19. How many owners' and directors' meetings are you prepared to attend for the management fee quoted? What fee do you propose to charge to attend any other meetings?

20. Do you provide 24 hour emergency service? How is this service provided? Is this included in the management fee?

21. What is the normal contract period in which you operate?

22. Provide details of the form of contract you use with other Management Companies, or contractors.

23. Are you a member of any professional trade bodies?

24. Can you provide references from other Management Companies for whom you act as Managing Agent?

Appendix D

List of Managing Agent's services

It's important for the Board of Directors to ascertain the services which the Managing Agent is prepared to provide for the management fee quoted, plus the additional costs of any other services. This list should be examined before interviewing potential Managing Agents, so that the directors can decide what services are important for their particular development.

Many of these services would be carried out in consultation with, and under the instructions of, the Board of Directors. It's important for the directors to decide which services require consultation and which don't.

This is also a useful check-list for directors to see if they're providing a good service to the apartment owners in cases where a Managing Agent isn't engaged. If you live in a self-managed development, how many of the services below are provided by your Board of Directors?

These are the possible services which a typical Managing Agent should be in a position to offer:

Maintenance and repair
- Prepare tenders, seek quotations and appoint the contractors required for routine maintenance and cleaning.
- Investigate the competence of all contractors and inspect their public liability insurance.
- Interview and select any full-time employees to be employed by the Management Company - caretakers, etc.
- Deal with all routine repairs and any scheduled and unscheduled cleaning and maintenance.
- Supervise all work carried on at the development.
- Keep a schedule of all equipment and machinery, arrange for annual service contracts where necessary and review them each year.
- Act as project manager for non-routine renewals, refurbishment and other works.
- Prepare a cyclical maintenance plan for all equipment.
- Deal with any matters in relation to security, break-ins or vandalism in the common areas.

Financial and accounting
- Maintain the Management Company bank accounts and reconcile the monthly statements.
- Maintain Service Charge accounts records for all owners.
- Carry out all bookkeeping functions.
- Prepare the annual budget and meet with the Board of Directors to finalise same, and provide a copy to each owner showing a detailed breakdown of costings.
- Apportion the Services Charges in accordance with the Lease.
- Manage the collection of Service Charges from all owners, including the collection of Service Charge arrears.
- Provide quarterly/monthly Direct Debit facilities to owners for payment of Service Charges.
- Examine and pay all contractor invoices.
- Liaise with the company auditor in relation to the annual accounts, and issue accounts documents to all owners prior to the Annual General Meeting.
- Advise the Board of Directors on the required level of Sinking Fund each year.
- Pay wages to Management Company employees, and deal with all PAYE and PRSI matters.
- Deal with the Revenue Commissioners in relation to all routine tax and accounting matters.

Legal and administration
- Advise the Board of Directors in relation to surveys of the development - Health & Safety, Fire, reinstatement valuations, etc. Circulate the results of the surveys to the directors.
- Deal with all professional and technical advisors.
- Negotiate the renewal of the insurance policies.
- Deal with all insurance claims if and when required.
- Deal with the Companies Office in relation to all routine company law matters.
- Liaise with the Board of Directors on the Annual General Meeting and circulate all owners with the Notice and Agenda, including statutory accounts documentation.
- Deal with all matters in relation to any Extraordinary General Meetings of the Management Company.
- Attend all General Meetings of the company, and meetings of

the Board of Directors, if necessary. Circulate all minutes of meetings as instructed by the Board of Directors.
- Deal with all breaches of the House Rules, Lease covenants, etc.
- Provide legal advice to the Board of Directors on routine matter relating to the Lease.
- Liaise with the Management Company solicitor if instructed to do so by the Board of Directors.
- Act as company secretary and carry out all functions of that position.
- Deal with any issues arising with the Local Authorities, adjoining neighbours, Gardaí, etc.
- Provide replies to Requisitions on Title when an owner is selling his apartment.
- Advise the Board of Directors on the most suitable location for the Health & Safety file, Title Deeds, company seal, etc.

General
- Maintain a diary of events and incidents at the development.
- Maintain computer database files in relation to all owners.
- Deal with all telephone and written communications from owners and residents in relation to all matter relevant to the remit and responsibilities of the Managing Agent.
- Issue a periodic newsletter to owners and/or occupiers.

Appendix E

Basic Management Company information with which the directors should be familiar

The directors of the Management Company should be familiar with all aspects of the management of the development, and compliance with company law. Here's a list - by no means exhaustive - of essential information which an incoming director to the Board should seek at the first directors' meeting after appointment:

- The contents of the Memorandum and Articles of Association of the company.
- The identity of the company:
    Solicitor
    Auditor
    Managing Agent
    Bank
    Insurance Broker
- Details of the Directors' and Officers' liability insurance cover.
- Details of all other insurance cover in the development.
- The contents of any surveyors' reports in relation to fire precautions, Health & Safety issues, reinstatement valuations, etc. The dates when these surveys are due to be carried out again.
- The location of the Title Deeds and Health & Safety file.
- The provisions in the Lease in relation to the duties and obligations of the Management Company.
- The identity of the signing authority for the company's bank accounts.
- The terms of the contract, if any, between the Managing Agent and the company.
- The position in relation to the collection of Service Charges from the owners, and the level of Service Charge arrears.
- Details of public liability insurance held by the various contractors in the development, including financial bonding where necessary.

Appendix F

Sample of House Rules & Emergency Contact Notice

1. All stereo, radio, TV and other appliances should be kept at a volume which will not disturb your neighbours or interfere with their quiet enjoyment of their home, and should not be audible outside your apartment between the hours of 10.30pm and 8.00am (or whatever other hours are stated in the Lease).
2. Car park spaces must only be used for the parking of private motor vehicles or motor cycles.
3. All entrance gates and doors to the common areas should be kept closed at all times. All doors should be closed quietly. All fire doors should be kept closed.
4. Strangers should not be allowed into the building or its environs at any time.
5. Please report any suspicious activity in the building or common areas to your nearest Garda Station (Location) – phone 123456
6. Do not place any obstructions (eg. bicycles, prams, baggage, etc.) in any of the common areas. Please do not litter any of the common areas.
7. No animal, bird or domestic pet that is likely to cause nuisance to the other occupiers is allowed to be kept in your apartment.
8. Washing or bedclothes should not be hung out from windows or balconies, and items such as flower boxes, etc. are not permitted outside on the window sills.
9. No alterations or building work is permitted in your apartment, nor any external decoration, without prior approval in writing from the Management Company.
10. All refuse must be placed in refuse sacks which should be securely tied and placed in the bin stores located in (location).
11. You are not permitted to erect television aerials or satellite dishes anywhere on the exterior of the building or balconies.
12. You are not permitted to place any signboards or placards of any kind in any window, or on the exterior of any part of the building or grounds, without the permission of the Management Company.
13. Owners should keep (Managing Agent) advised of telephone

numbers at which they may be contacted in the event of an emergency, and of the details of keyholders in the event of their absence on holidays, etc.

14. Smoking is forbidden by law in any of the internal common areas.

Emergency Telephone Numbers

Please remember to leave your name and contact number if you connect to an answering service.

Details	Contact	Phone details
All problems during normal working hours (also 24 hour messaging service)	(Managing Agent)	1234567
Electrical problems (in the common areas only) and Problems with the fire alarm system **which cannot wait until regular hours**	(Electrical Contractor)	(085) 1234567
Any problems in relation to water leaks or blocked drains **which cannot wait until regular hours**	(Mechanical Contractor)	(086) 1234567
Problems with car park gates or front door access	(Contractor)	(087) 1234567
Lifts	(Lift Contractor)	1800 1234567
Local Garda Station	(Location)	1234567
Local Fire Station	(Location)	1234567

Appendix G

Sample of a 'Service Charge Collection Policy' explanatory document

(This document should be amended and formulated to take into account the terms of the Lease for the development.)

Service Charge Collection Policy
at
ABC Apartments

The Board of Directors at ABC Apartments is acutely aware of the importance of collecting the Service Charges required for the running of the development and the administration of the Management Company. The non-payment of Service Charges by some apartment owners can cause serious cash flow problems, and the administration costs involved in pursuing those particular owners through the courts system can be considerable.

Each owner's Lease at ABC Apartments sets out very clearly the calculation of the Service Charges, the timeframe for paying them, and the action which can be taken against those owners who fail, neglect or refuse to pay the Service Charges. There are also provisions for the imposition of interest for the late payment of Service Charges.

The Board of Directors has therefore approved of the following procedures and regulations for the collection of the Service Charges at ABC Apartments:

1. Your Service Charge invoice will be sent to you, together with a copy of the budget, before the end of (insert relevant month) each year.

2. You must pay the Service Charges by (insert relevant date) under the terms of (insert relevant Section) of your Lease. Please note that our Managing Agent provides a facility whereby you can pay your Service Charges by quarterly/monthly direct debit if you prefer. There is no additional charge for this.

3. If you have not paid your Service Charges by (insert relevant date - about two weeks after the relevant date in section 2 above) the Managing Agent has been instructed to write to you, informing you that your Service Charges are overdue, and that interest is being applied to your Service Charge account at a rate of (insert relevant interest rate) in accordance with (insert relevant section) of the Lease. There will be a €(insert administration fee), plus VAT* administration fee payable by you for this letter, and this charge will be added to your Service Charge account.

4. If your Service Charges still remain unpaid on (insert relevant date - about two weeks after the relevant date in section 3 above) the Managing Agent has been instructed to write to you once again, informing you that your name, and the name of your lending institution, will be removed as interested parties from the block insurance policy if the Service Charge is not paid immediately. This action can be taken under the provisions of (insert relevant section) of your Lease. There will be a €(insert administration fee), plus VAT administration fee payable by you for this letter, and this charge will be added to your Service Charge account.

5. If your Service Charges remain unpaid on (insert relevant date - about two weeks after the relevant date in section 4 above) the Managing Agent has been instructed to send instructions to the insurance company to remove your name and that of your lending institution (if any), as interested parties, from the block insurance policy. This may result in you being unable to make any claims under the ABC Apartment's insurance policy. Your lending institution will also be informed that their name is being removed, as an interested party, from the insurance policy.

This action may become a very serious matter for you and therefore the Managing Agent has been instructed to write to you informing you that this action has been taken. There will be a €(insert administration fee), plus VAT administration fee payable by you for this letter, and this charge will be added to your Service Charge account. This fee also covers the administration cost of arranging to have your name and that of your lending institution removed as interested parties from the insurance policy, and reinstated as interested parties on the insurance policy when the arrears have been paid.

6. If your Service Charges are still unpaid on (insert relevant date - about four weeks after the relevant date in section 5 above) the matter will be referred to the Management Company's solicitor to institute legal proceedings against you for the forfeiture of your

Lease under (insert relevant section) of your Lease. The solicitor will also be notifying your lending institution about this matter. Any and all additional costs, both legal and administrative, incurred during the process of the legal proceedings will be charged to your Service Charge account under the provisions of (insert relevant section) of your Lease.

Please note that these regulations and procedures are being introduced immediately and they will be applied to all apartment owners. Please remember that if you are not in a position to pay the Service Charges in one lump sum, you can arrange through the Managing Agent to pay by quarterly/monthly Direct Debit.

We are aware that most owners at ABC Apartments have the best interests of ABC Apartments at heart, and pay the Service Charges on time. However, as with all apartment blocks, there is always a handful of people who blatantly disregard the rules and cause the Board of Directors and the Managing Agent great inconvenience in the process of trying to collect the Service Charges. It can also cause serious cash flow problems at ABC Apartments and this would be to the detriment of all apartment owners, as it can affect the carrying out of essential repairs, refurbishment, etc.

Although these regulations and procedures may appear to be strict, they have been devised with the best interests of ABC Apartments in mind.

This notice is issued under the provisions of (insert relevant section) of the Lease.

Approved by the Board of Directors at a meeting held on (insert relevant date).

* VAT on the administration fees must be charged if the person who is charging the fees is registered for VAT - ie. The Managing Agent.

Appendix H

Useful contacts

Companies Registration Office
Parnell House, 14 Parnell Square, Dublin 1
Phone: 1890 220226 / 01 8045200
Fax: 01 8045222
Email: info@cro.ie
Web: www.cro.ie
The main functions of the Companies Registration Office are to keep on public record all information in relation to incorporated companies and registered business names, and to enforce the Companies Acts in relation to the filing obligations of companies.

Health & Safety Authority
The Metropolitan Building, James Joyce Street, Dublin 1.
Phone: 1890 289389 / 01 6147000
Fax: 01 6147020
Email: wcu@hsa.ie
Web: www.hsa.ie
The Health & Safety Authority is the national body in Ireland with responsibility for securing a healthy and safe environment at work, providing information and advice to employers and employees on Health and Safety matters, and monitoring compliance with the relevant legislation.

Homebond
Construction House, Canal Road, Dublin 6.
Phone: 1850 306 300
Fax: 01 4966548
Web: www.homebond.ie
Many apartment structures are coved under the Homebond guarantee scheme. Homebond provides a warranty - subject to terms and conditions - in relation to major structural defects for a period of ten

years. Homebond has also produced a useful booklet in relation to tackling the causes of condensation in your home or apartment - see page 70.

National Consumer Agency
4 Harcourt Road, Dublin 2.
Phone: 1890 432432
Fax: 01 4025501
Web: www.nca.ie
  www.consumerconnect.ie

The function of the National Consumer Agency is to raise the profile of consumer issues and through information booklets and their website to inform consumers about current issues. The agency is playing an active role in the development of new regulations in the apartment management sector.

Office of the Director of Corporate Enforcement
16 Parnell Square, Dublin 1
Phone: 1890 315015 / 01 8585800
Fax: 01 8585801
Email: info@odce.ie
Web: www.odce.ie

The Office of the Director of Corporate Enforcement was established to encourage compliance by directors with the Companies Acts, to uncover and prosecute suspected breaches of company law and to commission and report formal company investigations.

Premier Guarantee
Phoenix House, 7/9 South Leinster Street, Dublin 2
Phone: 01 6616211
Web: www.coylehamiltonwillis.ie
  www.premierguarantee.co.uk

The Premier Guarantee is a structural insurance scheme which gives protection to homeowners in the event of serious structural problems for a period of ten years.

Index

In the subentries of the index, the following abbreviations are used:

A: Apartment
AA: Articles of Association
AGM: Annual General Meeting
BoD: Board of Directors
D: Developer
EGM: Extraordinary General Meeting
L: Lease
MA: Managing Agent
MAA: Memorandum & Articles of Association
MC: Management Company
PG: Private 'gated' development
SC: Service Charge

'$^A/_Z$' method of Service Charge apportionment, 86
Access, to A by MC, 54
Access, to MC books of account, 103
Accidental damage, insurance against, 136
Accounts - see also bank accounts. In Requisitions on Title, 18; control of, by BoD, 28, 30; financial statements in, 31; audit of, 31, 102; disclosure of director's interest in contracts in, 85; financial year of, 100-101; shortfall in Year 2, 102; annual accounts, 102-103, 112, 116; in PG, 103-104; in AA, 107
Activities, of MC, in MAA, 106-107
Ad-hoc owners' committee, 12, 13-14
Administration fees, 46, 48; for non payment of SC, 55, 91-97; charged to owner-landlord, 129
Advertisement, exhibiting in A window, 49-50
Aerials, prohibition on erection of, 48
Alarms, 46-47; keyholders to have codes for, 61; cost of, in private house, 82
"All That and Those....", 22
Alternative accommodation, insurance to provide for, 136
Amending the Articles of Association - see Articles of Association
Animals, keeping in A, 48-49; kept in unsuitable conditions, 49
Annual Budget - see also supplementary budget. 73-81; initial calculations of, by MA, 9; BoD duty to prepare, 30; MA fees in, 32; security upgrade in, 62; budget headings, 78-80; errors in calculation of, 81; deficit, 81; provision for Sinking Fund in, 83; owner's disagreement with, 88; fraud in, 88; owner's challenge to, 88; owner's right to obtain details of, 90, 92; MA refusal to provide details of, to owners, 90; in PG, 103-104; struck too low by BoD, 114
Annual General Meeting - see also first Annual General Meeting. 121-122, 142; changing BoD decisions at, 54; owner getting elected to BoD at, 88; voting rights of owners at, 98-99, 108-110; approval of annual accounts at, 102-103; BoD duty to convene, 112, 116; appointment, removal and rotation of BoD at, 115-116; BoD first meeting af-

ter, 119; amending AA at, 123; Agenda of, 121

Annual maintenance contracts, lifts, 69; in initial budget, 75; in annual budget, 78; in PG, 103-104

Annual Return, 142; BoD duty to file, 30, 102-103, 116, 120, 123-124; BoD failure to file, 114

Anti-social hours, emergency callouts, 70

Anti-social neighbours, 57; tenants, 58, 130

'Any other business', at AGM, 121-122, 123

Apartment Lease - see Lease

Apartment, ownership of, 1, 22-25; don't own freehold, 1; Lease drawn by d, 5; snags in, 13; buying a new, 5, 18, 100-101, 150-155; buying second-hand, 17, 18, 133, 98, 150-155; SC arrears on, 17, 98; Requisitions on Title, 18; description of, in L, 22; walls of, 23; balconies of, 23; ceilings and floors of, 23; windows and doors of, 23; glass in, 23-24; duty to keep in good decorative order, 42; noise in, 43-47; parties in, 46; birds or animals in, 48; signs placed in windows of, 49-50; letting bedroom in, 50; use of, as single private residence, 51; structural alterations to, 52; painting exterior of, 52; permit access to, by MC, 54; BoD authority to force entry to, 55; security in, 62; water leak in, 69; damp, 70; on ground floor, lift costs, 80-81; as 'first rung on property ladder', 84; selling, with inadequate Sinking Fund, 84; floor area of, to apportion SC, 86; number of bedrooms in, to apportion SC, 86; SC on new, 100-101; SC for unsold or unoccupied, 102; decrease in value of, due to lack of repairs, 114; selling, when MC is struck-off, 124; ownership of, retained by D, 125-126; displaying copies of House Rules in, 130; renting out, 129-130

Apportionment of Service Charge, 86

Architect's Completion Certificate, 15

Architect's plans, BoD to keep copy, 29

Arrears - see Service Charges

Articles of Association, 106-107; resignation of directors in, 16; responsibilities of MC in, 34; amending, by owners, 108, 117, 122-123; amending, by owners, to appoint or dismiss MA, 38, 57, 77, 123; amending, by owners, to change BoD decisions, 54, 88; amending, by owners to ensure better budget details, 77, 123; voting rights of owners in, 98-99, 109, 109, 121; amending, by owners, for access to MC books of account, 103; voting rights of subscribers in, 109-110, 123; appointment, removal and rotation of directors in, 115-116; further provisions to disqualify a director from acting in, 117; procedures for General Meetings in, 122

Auctioneer, first budget, 76

Auctioneer's signs, 49-50

Audit, BoD to arrange, 31, 112; fees, in annual budget, 79, 83

Auditor, report of, in annual accounts, 102-103; filing Annual Return, 102, 123; as company secretary, 120; report of, at AGM, 121; appointment and remuneration of, at AGM, 121

Backhanders, to MA, 35

Balance sheet, of MC, 121

Balcony, 23, 25; responsibility for, 29; hanging clothes on, 48; regulations for use of, 51-52; structural alterations to, 53

Bank accounts of Management Company, 73, 99-100; Sinking Fund, 83; control of, 100; signatures on, 100

Bank charges, in annual budget, 79

Bank standing order, payment of SC by, 85, 87

Bathrooms, fitting linoleum on floors, 50

Bedclothes, in window or on balcony, 48

Bedrooms, number of, to apportion SC, 86

Bicycles, 68-69

Bike sheds, 7, 9, 25, 68; BoD power to relocate, 54; in car park, 80

Bin stores, 7, 9, 25, dumping of non-domestic refuse in, 29; impractical location of, 43; BoD power to relocate, 54; in car park, 80

Birds, keeping in A, 48-49

Block insurance policy, 135-136, 142; in Requisitions on Title, 18; cost of, in annual budget, 79; removal of owner and lending institution as interested parties from, 93-96

Board of Directors, 110-119, 142; first, nominated by D, 5, 10, 109, 115; election of, by owners, 10, 15, 16, 77, 105, 107, 110, 115, 121; taking control of, by owners at first AGM, 12, 126, 116; first BoD resigns, 15, 16, 109, 115, 126; owners elect after D's transfer of interests, 16, 110, 118-119; decision of, to engage MA, 16-17, 31, 112; demands SC arrears from new owner, 17, 98; in PG, 19, 39; manages on behalf of MC, 27, 88, 110, 115; company law compliance, 27, 102-103, 110, 111-112, 116; duties and responsibilities of, 28-31, 110, 111-112; civil claim against, for negligence, 31, 138-139; dismisses MA, 31, 38, 57; replaces MA, 31; manages without MA, 31-32; loses control to MA, 33; instructs MA, 33; as executive managers of development, 34; makes all management decisions, 34; delegates routine issues to MA, 34, 112; half-hearted and disinterested, 34; dissatisfaction with MA, 35; member of, causing aggravation to MA, 37; appoints MA, 38-39, 112; duty of, to charge interest, 42, 93; instructs MA to remove aerials and satellite dishes, 48; makes regulations re common areas, 49, 53; grants approval for signs, 50; gives permission for structural alterations, 52; refusal to allow structural alterations, 53; makes car park rules, 54; carries out work in A, 54; forces entry to A, 55; levies administration fees against owner, 55, 91-97; institutes legal proceedings against owner for forfeiture of L, 56; informs owner's lending institution of forfeiture proceedings, 57; owners seek change of, at General Meeting, 57, 77; introduces supplementary budget, 62, 71, 81; duty of, to maintain common areas, 71; manages 'business' of MC, 73, 88, 110, 111, 115, 138-139; approves annual budget, 73-74; duty of, to levy Service Charges, 74, 90; holds informal owners' meeting to discuss budget, 74; decides on Sinking Fund, 76; duty of, to act in accordance with MAA, 77, 115, 122; no power to alter L, 81; decides on annual budget, 82; inadequate Sinking Fund, 84, 114; seeks written quotations where MA has interest in contracts, 84; apportions SC among owners, 86; collects SC, 87, 92-97; owner getting elected onto, 88, 117-118, 138-139; not obliged to consult owners, 88, 115; chases SC arrears, 89, 92-97; authority of, to implement 'SC collection policy', 91-97; no duty to provide any service to owner with SC arrears, 94, 140; duty of, to insure, 94, 134; signatures of, on bank accounts, 100; duty of, to file annual return, 102-103, 116, 123; access of, to MC books of account, 103, 112, 120; members of, must understand company law, 106, 111; duties and rights of, in AA, 107; dismissal of, in AA, 107, 115; director can be non-member of MC, 110; duty of, to act as fiduciaries, 111; duty of, to act in best interests of MC, 111, 115, 138-139; inexperienced and voluntary nature of, 111, 138-139; duty of, to manage with skill and diligence, 111, 118, 138-139; duty of, to safeguard assets of MC, 112; duty of, to maintain company registers, 112, 116; duty of, to divulge interest in contracts, 112; duty of, to convene General Meetings of MC, 112, 116, 122; duty of, to retain minutes of meetings, 29, 110, 112; duty of, to ensure competence of contractors, 112; penalties and sanctions against, 112; liability of, to fines and imprisonment, 112-113; defence of inexperience, 113, 138-139; civil liabilities of, 113-115; members of, personally exposed to litigation, 114, 138-139;

powers of, 115; appointment, removal and rotation of, 115-116; death of director, 115; re-election of, 116, 126; joins in signing of every L, 116-117, 126; signs MC Agreement, 117; disqualification of director, 117; workload of, if no MA engaged, 118; meetings of, 118-119; gives instructions to company secretary, 119; ensures competence of company secretary, 120, 123; authority of, to call EGM, 122; liability of, at strike-off, 124, 125; refusal of, to sign L, 126; as employer under Health & Safety regulations, 128; duty of, to carry out fire safety survey, 128; duty of, to act on complaints from tenants, 130; considers taking in charge in PG, 130-131; use of insurance broker, 133; duty of, to ensure proper reinstatement valuation, 135; allows owners to decide insurance policy excess, 139-140; essential information for, about MC, 161

Boilers, engineering insurance for, 137

Books of account, BoD to maintain, 30, 102, 116; access to, 103; MA refusal to hand over, 103, 120; BoD fails to maintain, 113

Breach of contract by developer, 127

Breaches of corporate rules by officers of MC, owners' right to redress, 108; courts powers, 112

Breaches of House Rules by tenant, 58, 129

Breaches of owners' obligations in L, BoD duty to take action, 30; MA issues letters re, 34; legal proceedings by BoD against owner for, 52-53; owner indemnifies MC against, 55, 91; remedies for, 56; covenants by MC and D, 56; MA refusal to take action for, 57; failure to pay SC, 87-92

Budget - see annual budget and supplementary budget

Bulbs, replacement of, 34; cost of, in annual budget, 78

'Business' of the Management Company, 73, 106-107, 108, 111

Buying a new apartment, **5**; Requisitions on Title, 18; SC apportionment, 100-101; checklist when buying, 150-155

Buying a second-hand apartment, 17; Requisitions on Title, 18; insurance claims history, 133; checklist when buying, 150-155

Capital expenditure in budget, 73, 80

Car parking, 64-68; space, described in L, 22; licence to use, 22; under control of MC, 25; regulations in L for, 43, 66; commercial vehicles, 43, 66; letting car space separately, 51, 67; BoD making regulations for, 54, 65; marking car spaces, 54, 65, 66; unallocated spaces, 64; allocated spaces, 65; access to car park, 66; car space too small, 67; obstruction of car space, 67; stolen vehicles in car park, 68; in PG, 72; cost of, in annual budget, 80; SC for, 86-87

Caretaker, 28; in annual budget, 78; as employee of MC, 127-128

Carpet cuttings, disposal of, 43

Carpets, shaking from window, 48

Cash flow statement, 121

'Caveat emptor' - let the buyer beware, 76

CCTV, replacement of, 28, 83; cost of, 62, 83; annual maintenance contract for, 78

Ceilings of apartment, 23

Checklist when appointing MA, 156-157

Checklist when buying apartment, 150-155

Chewing gum, removal of, 64

Circuit Court, legal proceedings against owner in, 52-53; forfeiture of L in, 56; summons for forfeiture, 59; legal proceedings by owner against BoD for removal from insurance in, 95

Cisterns in apartment, 24

Civil liability of Board of Directors, 113 - 115

Clamping companies, hiring by BoD, 54, 65; owners contacting, 65

Cleaning, duties of BoD, 28, 62-63, 118; after parties, 46; graffiti, 63-64; equipment, annual maintenance contract for,

78; in annual budget, 78

Clothes, in window or on balcony, 48

Collection of Service Charges - see Service Charges

Commercial activity, in apartment, 51

Commercial vehicles, in car park, 43, 66

Commission on contracts, paid to MA, 35

Committee of owners - see ad-hoc owners' committee.

Common areas, 25, 143; right to travel through, 7; owned by D, 7; D's duty to maintain, 8; D transfers ownership of, 14; freehold of, in PG, 19; walls, 23; common area installations, 24; BoD duty to maintain, 28, 62, 71; BoD plan to upgrade, 28, 83; BoD to keep adequately lighted, 29; signs placed in, 49; BoD makes regulations re, 49, 53; bicycles in, 68; structural problems in, 71; refurbishment of, 83, replacement of floor coverings in, 83; owners' property interest in, 105; person killed or injured in, 128; damage done to, by tenants, 129; insurance of, in PG, 140

Common electrical and plumbing installations, right to be connected to, 7; in PG, 26; BoD plan for replacement of, 28; BoD to keep schedule of, 29

Common facilities, MC responsibility to repair, 22

Communication breakdown, between BoD and MA, 37

Companies Acts, BoD omissions under, 113

Companies Office, 167; BoD duty to file Annual Return in, 30, 102-103; inadequate records in self-managed developments, 32; power of, to restore struck-off MC, 125; issues warnings before strike-off, 125

Company directors - see Board of Directors

Company law, MC compliance with, 8, 27, 102-103, 112, 119 ; in PG, 19; costs of, 83, 124; members of BoD must understand, 106, 111; BoD must manage MC under, 110, 111, 115; BoD fails to comply with, 112; breach of, by D, 127

Company legal structure, 19, 106

Company limited by guarantee, 105

Company limited by shares, 105

Company registers, BoD to maintain, 30; kept at registered office of MC, 106

Company restoration - see restoration

Company seal, 106

Company secretary, 143; BoD to appoint, 30; fees of, in annual budget, 79, 83; duty of, to file Annual Return, 102-103; 119-120, 123; liability of, at strike-off, 124, 125; in PG, 130

Company strike-off - see strike-off

Completion Certificate, 15

Completion of development, owner to take action for, 11, 12

Compressors, engineering insurance for, 137

Condensation in apartment, 70

Conduits, connect to common installations, 24

Contact information, owners', 59-60; key-holders', 61; tenants', 61

Contractors, BoD appoints, 28, 112, 118; insurance cover of, 28, 136; MA dismisses, 33; MA appoints, 34; twenty-four hour emergency cover, 69; written quotations from, 76, 84; annual maintenance contracts, 78; contracts, MA interest in, 84-85; contracts, director's interest in, 85, 112; contracts, fraud in awarding, 88, BoD duty to ensure competence of, 112; Health & Safety with, 127-128; MA checks insurances of, 136

Contractor's waste, disposal of, 43

Corridors, 25

Courts, referral to, in noise disputes, 45; in running business from A, 51; in balcony misusage, 52; in unauthorised structural alterations, 52; presume members of BoD understand company law, 106, 113; discretion to disqualify directors, 112

Covenants in the Lease, 143

Credit forward on Service Charge accounts,

100-101
Criminal offences committed by BoD, 112
Current account - see bank account
Damages awarded by courts, 56-57
Damp apartments, 70
Dangerous materials rule, 53
Deposit account - see bank account
Developer, 143; buys land to develop, 5; forms MC, 5, 109, 110; nominates subscribers, 5, 109; nominates BoD, 5,10, 110, 115; signs MC Agreement, 5; agrees to transfer interests, 5; as Lessor, 7; covenants to manage development, 7, 8, 88, 98; owns common areas, 7; appoints MA, 9; obligations in L, 8-9, duty of, to insure, 8; calculates initial budget, 9, 75, 76; slow to complete development, 10; responsible for snagging, 10,11; invitation to first owners' meeting, 13; pressure by ad-hoc committee, 14; transfers his interests to MC, 14-15, 110, 116, 117; arranges first General Meeting after transfer, 16; refuses to transfer interest, 17, 125-127; responsibility to manage development, 27, 116, 126; dismisses MA, 37, 57; refuses to dismiss MA, 37; long-term contract with MA, 38; covenant of, re breaches of Lease by owners, 56, 98; no obligations re security, 61; duty of, to approve budget, 74; instructs MA to make first budget low, 75; decides the apportionment of SC among A's, 86; collects SC arrears, 97-98; first bank accounts in name of, 99-100; SC of unsold A's, 102; controls MC through subscribers, 109; completes MC Agreement, 117; implied term in L to sell all A's, 127; arranges initial insurances, 134
Direct debit, payment of SC by, 85, 87
Director of Corporate Enforcement, 168; owner's right to contact, 108; can inspect minutes of directors' meetings, 112, 119; application to courts by, for sanctions against BoD, 113, 138; may inspect other companies, 113; can compel the holding of an AGM, 121, 126

Directors - see Board of Directors
Directors' and Officers' liability insurance, 31, 138-139; in annual budget, 79, 139; in PG, 140
Directors' report, in annual accounts, 102-103, at AGM, 121
Director's interest in contracts, 85
Director's interests in other companies, 30
Disqualification of directors, 112, 117
District Court, in noise disputes, 45, 47
Dogs in apartment, 48-49
Domestic animals in apartment, 48-49
Domestic appliances, disposal of, 43
Domestic refuse - see also non-domestic refuse. BoD duty to manage, 29, 42; owners' duty to dispose of, 42; BoD issues refuse bags, 43; leaving, on balcony, 52; in PG, 72; in annual budget, 79; cost of, in private house, 82
Doors, in A, 23, responsibility for, 29; entrance, broken, 69, 71
Drains, 24; in PG, 26
Dublin City Council, "Successful Apartment Living, Part 2" report, 128
Duplex, definition of, 86; apportionment of SC in, 86
Duvets, shaken from window, 48
Easements, 24, 105, 143; in PG, 26
Electrical problems, 24
Electricity bills in annual budget, 79
Emergency contacts, 69-70, sample of notice, 162-163
Emergency, 69-70; BoD authority to force entry to A in, 55
Employees of Management Company, under Health & Safety regulations, 127-128
Employer, definition of, under Health & Safety regulations, 128
Employers' liability insurance, 136; BoD duty to arrange, 31; in PG, 140
Engineering insurance, 137; BoD duty to arrange, 31, 69; in annual budget, 79; in PG, 140
Entrance gates, 25, 69, 71; annual maintenance contract for, 78; replacement of,

in Sinking Fund, 83
Entrance sign, responsibility of D, 9
Environmental Protection Agency Act, 1992, re noise, 45, 47
Equitable ownership, 3
Estate Rules, in PG, enforcement of, 39
Estate, definition of, in L, 143-144
European Standard EN50131-1 of 1997, re alarms, 47
Excess on insurance policy, 31, 133, 139-140
Excessive weight rule, 53
Exterior, decoration of, 52-53
Extraordinary General Meetings - see also General Meetings. 120, 122, 144; change BoD decisions at, 54; to decide car parking regulations, 65; owners call, to dismiss MA, 77; owners call, to improve management, 88; voting rights of owners at, 98-99, 108-110; BoD duty to convene, 112
Facilities manager, MA as, 34
Falling objects, insurance against, 136
Fiduciaries, BoD duty to act as, 111
Financial bonding, BoD to check, 30, 114
Financial matters, 73-104
Financial statements, BoD duty to prepare, 31
Financial year of Management Company for accounts, 100-101
Fines, levied against BoD, 112, 128
Fire, insurance against, 136
Fire brigade charges, insurance against, 136
Fire Certificates, 15
Fire Department, alarm deactivation, 47
Fire extinguishers, plan for periodic maintenance, 28
Fire Officer, 11
Fire safety, 128-129
Fire alarms, plan for periodic maintenance of, 28; commissioning certificates for, 29; annual maintenance contracts for, 78
First Annual General Meeting - see also Annual General Meeting. 121, 126; election of BoD at, 10, 126; owners take control of BoD at, 12, 116, 126; holding of, 16, 126; resignation of BoD at, 16, 126; in PG, 19
First bank accounts of Management Company, 99-100
First budget in new development, 75
Flat-pack furniture packaging, disposal of, 43
Flood, insurance against, 136
Floodlights, BoD power to switch off, 54
Floor area of apartment used to apportion SC, 86
Floors, 23; wooden, 50; coverings, in common areas, 83
'For Sale' signs, 49-50
Forfeiture of Lease, legal proceedings against owner for, 56, 58, 96
Fraud in awarding service contracts, 88; re BoD, 112
Freehold, 144; compared to Leasehold, 2; ownership of house in PG, 4, 19; D's original ownership of, 5, 7; D transfers ownership of, 14; MC owns, 16; of common areas in PG, 19; owner's interest in PG, 26
Gardaí, alarm deactivation, 47; investigation of accident in common areas, 128
Gates, plan for periodic maintenance of, 28; commissioning certificates, 29
General Meetings of Management Company - see also Annual General Meeting (AGM) and Extraordinary General Meeting (EGM). D arranges, after transfer of interests, 15 - 16, 120-122, 144; to amend AA, 38; owners seek change of BoD, 57, 116; voting rights of owners at, 98-99, 108-110, 121; appointment of BoD at, 105, 116; in AA, 107; BoD duty to convene, 112; resolutions at, 121-122; in PG, 130
Glass, in windows of A, 23-24, responsibility for, 29; replacement of, 34
Governing committee, 144. See Board of Directors.

Graffiti in common areas, 63-64
Gym, 25
Health & Safety, 71, 127-128; file, 29; D hands over file to MC, 15, contents of file, 15; keep file in safe place, 15; contractors to comply with regulations, 28; in annual budget, 79, 83; in PG, 130
Health & Safety Authority, 11, 128, 167
Health & Safety Certificates, D hands over, 15
Health and Safety statement, 29
High Court, owner's right to apply to, 108; authority of, to restore struck-off MC, 125
Homebond, 70, 167
House Rules and Emergency Contact Notice, sample, 162-163
House Rules, 144; enforcement of, 7, 28; owner's covenants in L to comply with, 25, 28; MA issues letters for breach of, 34; definition of, 41; disposal of domestic waste in, 42; breaches of, by tenants, 58, 129; notice also displays emergency contacts, 70; copy of, in rented A's, 130; sample notice for display in common areas, 162-163
House, in PG, 71
Implied terms of Lease, owner liable for expenses in event of breach, 56, 91-92; BoD to introduce supplementary budgets, 81; D will try to sell all A's, 127
Imprisonment, BoD liable to, 112, 128
Indemnify Management Company, duty of owner to, 55-56
Initial budget in new development, 75-76
Insurance - see also block insurance, property owners' liability insurance, employers' liability insurance, engineering insurance, Directors' & Officers liability insurance. 133-140; common areas of PG, 19, 140; contractors, 28; BoD duty to insure, 31, 134; claims, 31; excess on claims, 31, 133, 139; inadequate, in self-managed developments, 32; additional risks, by action of owner, 53; in annual budget, 79; in private house, 82; removal of owner and lending institution as interested parties from policy, 93-96, 140; inadequate, 114; owner entitled to copy of policy, 133; claims history, 133; at startup, 134; reinstatement valuation, 134-135; owners' individual cover, 137-138; premium payment plan, 139; in PG, 140

Insurance broker, BoD duty to supply information, 31; instructions to, from MA to remove interested parties from block policy, 93-96; use of, 133

Interest on Service Charge arrears, 30, 42, 93

Interested parties on insurance policy, removal of owner and lending institution, 93-96; 140

Invoices, MA to pay, 34

Irish Society for the Prevention of Cruelty to Animals, 49

Joists, ceilings in A, 23

Keyholders, 47, 61

Keys, cost of, in annual budget, 78

Kickbacks, to MA, 35

Kitchen, fitting linoleum on floors of, 50

Landscaping, BoD plan to upgrade, 28; BoD responsible for, 62, 118; equipment, annual maintenance contract for, 78; in annual budget, 78; cost of, in private house, 82

Landscaping, completion of, 9; expenses, in initial budget, 75; cost of, in private house, 81

Law Society of Ireland, 98

Leaks in apartment, 13

Lease, 2, 144-145; for long period, 3; drawn up by D's solicitor, 5; copy of, 6, 17; covenants by D in, 8-9, 98; D's right to appoint MA in, 9; no provision in, for ad-hoc committee, 14; assignment of, to new buyer, 17; details of A ownership in, 22; description of A in, 22; map attached to, 22; car space in, 22; balconies in, 23; ceilings in, 23; floors in, 23; windows in, 23; doors in, 23; responsibility for glass in, 23-24; owner's right to connect to common installations in, 24; owner's right to quiet life in, 24-25; retained lands in, 25; BoD duties in, 28-31; BoD duty re breaches of rules in, 30; BoD to calculate SC in accordance with, 30; rules in, 41; owner's duties and obligations in, 42-56; owner's duty to pay rent in, 42; owner's duty to disposal of domestic waste in, 42; owner's duty to pay SC in, 42; owner's duty to repair and decorate A in, 42; car park rules in, 53, 66; noise rules in, 43-47; aerials and satellite dish rules in, 48; clothes in A windows in, 48; clothes on balconies in, 48; domestic animals and birds in A, in, 48-49; signposts and advertisements in, 49-50; 'For Sale' and 'To Let' signs in, 49-50; wooden floors in, 50-51; letting part only of premises in, 51; use as single private residence in, 51; balcony rules in, 51-52; structural alterations in, 52-53; decorate exterior of A in, 52-53; excessive weight rule in, 53; dangerous materials rule in, 53; access to A by MC in, 54; nuisance rule in, 55; owner to indemnify MC in, 55-56, 90; implied terms of, 56; legal proceedings for forfeiture of, 56, 58, 96; provision for contact information in, 61; bicycles in, 68; car park costs in, 80; BoD no power to alter, 81; provision for supplementary budget in, 81; SC collection method in, 85; SC apportionment must be in accordance with, 86; BoD duty to levy SC in, 90; administration fees in, 91; BoD duty to impose interest in, 92; BoD under no duty to provide service to owner with SC arrears in, 94, 140; no provision for SC in unsold A's in, 102; BoD acts subject to terms of, 115; provisions in, for transfer by D, 125; signing of, 126; implied term of, that D will sell all A's, 127; breaches of, by tenant, 129; BoD duty to insure in, 134

Leasehold, 145; compared to freehold, 2; interest of owner, 105

Legal fees, in annual budget, 79

Legal matters, 105-132

Legal proceedings, by BoD against owner for breach of L, 52-53; for forfeiture of L, 56, 96; against BoD by owner for removal from insurance policy, 94-96; by BoD against owner for SC arrears, 96-97; by D against owners with SC arrears, 97-98; by owner against D for mismanagement, 98

Legal structure of apartment development, necessity for, 19, 106

Lending institution, informed about forfeiture proceedings, 57, 59, 96; removal as interested party from insurance policy, 93-96

Lessee, 145. See owner

Lessor, 145. See developer

Letting apartment - see renting out

Letting part only of premises, 51

Lifts, 25, 71; plan for periodic maintenance, 28; replacement of, 28, 83; commissioning certificates, 29; engineering insurance, 31, 137; annual maintenance contracts, 69, 78; phones in, in annual budget, 79; apportionment of costs of, 80-81; statutory inspection certificates, 137

Light sleeping neighbours, 44

Lighting, plan for periodic maintenance, 28; BoD duties re, 29, 71

Limited company legal structure, 19, 105, 106, 124

Locks, replacement of, 34; cost of, in annual budget, 78

Maintenance contracts - see annual maintenance contracts.

Maintenance of development, BoD's duty, 28-31

Management committee, 145. See Board of Directors

Management Company Agreement, 5 145; D's duty to complete, 8; completion of, 14, 116-117

Management Company, 145-146; formation of by D, 5; owner becoming member of, 6; signs Lease at sale closing, 8, 116; ensures corporate compliance, 8, 102-103, 116, 119; takes over D's responsibilities, 15; first General Meeting of, after D's transfer, 16; owns freehold and reversionary interests, 16; controlled by owners, 16; name of, in Requisitions on Title, 18; MAA of, in Requisitions on Title, 18; accounts of, in Requisitions on Title, 18; claims on funds in Requisitions of Title, 18; legal structure of, 19, 105; membership of, in PG, 19, 130; responsibilities of, in PG, 19, 26; responsibility of, for repairs, 22; duty of, to maintain balconies, 23; responsibility of, for walls, 23; responsibility of, for windows and doors, 23; responsibility of, for glass, 23-24; duty of, to clean common area windows, 24; responsibility of, for conduits and pipes, 24; covenant of, to ensure quiet life, 25; BoD manages on behalf of, 27, 110; administration of, 29; General Meetings of, 29, 116, 120; BoD maintains ledgers of, 29, 116; BoD maintains members' register of, 30, 116; bank accounts of, 30, 99-100, 116; books of account of, 30, 73, 102-103, 116; financial statements of, 31, 102-103; audit of, 31, 102-103, 116; BoD must act in best interests of, 53, 111; right of access to A's, 54; expenses and outlay of, re breach of L by owner, 55; covenants of, re breaches of Lease, 56; BoD manages 'business' of, 73, 108; MA interest in contracts with, 84-85; director's interest in contracts with, 85; limited powers of member of, 88, 108; risk of court proceedings against, re 'SC collection Policy', 90; voting rights of owners who owe money to, 98-99; annual accounts of, 102-103, 116; Annual Return of, 102-103, 116, 120; access to books of account of, 103; accounts of, in PG, 103-104; property interest of members of, 105; registered office of, 106; MAA of, 106-107; D's control of, through subscribers, 109; directors of, 110-119; penalties and sanctions against BoD of, 112-113; civil liability of BoD of, 113-115; has no authority until D completes MC Agreement, 116; company secretary of, 119-120; penalties against, for not filing Annual Return, 123; strike-off of, 124-125; assets of, vest in Minister for Finance at strike-off, 124; owners take over, at first AGM, 126-127; essential information about, for BoD, 160

Management of development, 27 - 40; responsibility of D, 27; without MA, 31-32; unsuitability of company structure for, 106; owners' control over, 108; must be done by BoD under MAA, 110, 111; powers of BoD, 115; insurance claims history, 133

Managing Agent, 31-40, 146-147; D's appointment of, at beginning, 8; duties of, 9; as agent of D, 9,11; calculation of initial budget, 9; problems at startup, 10; completion of snagging list, 10; powers over D, 11; pays for snagging, 11; establishes ad-hoc owners' committee, 12; not responsible for snags in individual A, 13; calling first owners' meeting, 13; benefit of ad-hoc committee to, 14; refusal of, to hand over Health & Safety file, 15; position of, after D's transfer, 16-17; name of, in Requisitions on Title, 18; contract of, in Requisitions on Title, 18; fee of, in Requisitions on Title, 18; carries out management functions, 27; BoD authority to appoint, 30, 38, 112, 38-39; fees of, 32; role of, 33-35; commission on contracts, 35; dissatisfaction with, 35; standard of service of, 35; fees of, too low, 36; dismissal of, 36-38, 57, 123; terms of contract of, 38; response times of, 39; in PG, 39; breaches of rules by tenants, 41; deals with non-domestic waste, 43; role of, in noise disputes, 45; deals with parties, 46; removes aerials and satellite dishes, 48; role of, in birds and animals disputes, 49; grants approval for signs, 50; levies administration fees for breaches of House Rules, 55, 129; refusal of, to take action for breach of L, 57; contacts owner-landlord of troublesome tenants,

58; problems contacting owners, 59-60; circulates cleaning schedule to occupiers, 63; investigates poor water pressure, 64; removes bicycles, 68; provides emergency contacts, 69; common area repairs, 71; prepares annual budget, 73-74, 76; instructed by D to make first budget low, 75-76; seeks quotations from contractors for budget, 76; holds informal owners' budget meeting, 77; fee of, for unscheduled visits, 79; project management fees, 79; fees, in annual budget, 80, 83; interest in contracts, 84-85; provides SC payment facilities, 85; advises D on apportionment of SC, 86; collects SC, 87, 92-97; not obliged to consult owners, 88; chases SC arrears, 89, 93-97; fee of, insufficient to chase defaulters, 89; refusal of, to provide budget details with SC invoice, 90; charges administration fees, 91-97; 'SC collection Policy' of, 92-97; must take instructions from D, 97-98; first MC bank accounts in name of, 99-100; control of MC bank accounts, 100; signatures of, on MC bank accounts, 100; refusal of, to hand over MC books of account to BoD, 103, 120; fees in PG, 103-104; BoD must ensure competence of, 112; incompetence of, liability of BoD, 114; professional indemnity insurance of, 114; acts as company secretary, 120; as employer under Health & Safety regulations, 128; supplies copy of insurance policy to owner, 133; arranges original insurances, 134; checks insurances of contractors, 136; checklist when appointing, 156-157; list of potential services available from, 158-160; furnishes MC details to potential buyer, 151

Map attached to L, 22

Mats, shaking from window, 48

Mechanical and electrical drawings, BoD to keep copy of, 29

Meeting, informal owners', to discuss budget, 74, 77, 84; to discuss car space marking, 67; to decide on insurance policy excess, 139-140

Meetings of directors, 118-119; minutes of, 119

Member of Management Company - see also owner; 6, 10, 107-110, 147; in PG, 19, 130; details of, in company register, 30; limited powers of, 88, 108; property interests of, 105; appoint BoD at General Meeting of MC, 105; limited liability of, 106; duties and rights of, in AA, 107; in PG, 130

Membership Certificate, 7, 17; BoD duty to issue, 30, 120

Memorandum and Articles of Association of Management Company, 106-107, 147; in Requisitions on Title, 18; subscribers to, 5, 109; BoD manages development in accordance with, 111; company secretary ensures compliance with, 119

Mice, 28

Minister of Finance, assets of MC vest in, at strike-off, 124

Minority rights, suppression of, 110, 127

Minutes of meetings, BoD duty to retain, 112

Musical instruments, playing in A, 44

National Consumer Agency, 168

National Standards Authority alarm specifications, 47

Neighbours, noise disputes, 44; birds and animals disputes, 49; troublesome, how to deal with, 57;

Newsletters, cost of, in annual budget, 79

Noise, duties of occupier in L, 43-47; standards in Ireland, 45; parties, 46; alarms, 46-47; wooden floors, 50

'Non-domestic' environment, in Health & Safety regulations, 127

Non-domestic refuse - see also domestic refuse. Disposal of, 29, 43

Non-Fatal Offences Against the Person Act, 1997, 128

Nuisance, occupier to refrain from, 55; noise, 43

Occupiers, breach of House Rules, 34;

duties and obligations in L, 42-56; disposal of domestic waste, 42; use of car park, 53; noise restrictions, 43-47; not to erect aerials and satellite, 48; not to hang clothes in A windows, 48; not to hang clothes on balconies, 48; domestic animals and birds in A, 48-49; not to display signposts and advertisements, 49-50; not to let out part only of premises, 51; use A as single private residence, 51; use of balcony, 51-52; prohibition of excessive weight, 53; prohibition of dangerous materials, 53; allow access to A by MC, 54; not to cause nuisance, 55

Officers of Management Company - see also Board of Directors and company secretary. 147; breaches of corporate rules by, 108

Ordinary resolution at General Meetings, 116

Overdue Service Charges - see Service Charges

Own-door duplex, in annual budget, 81; apportionment of SC in, 86

Owner - see also member of Management Company. Reference throughout book, 3; entitled to copy of L, 6; what owner buys, 7, 105; obligations of, 7, 42-56; as member of MC, 7, 107-110, 10; influence of, at startup, 10; elects BoD, 10, 15, 16, 105, 107, 108, 110, 116; startup problems for, 10; takes action re snagging, 11, 12; withholds SC, 12, 87-90; takes control of BoD at first AGM, 12, 116, 126; ad-hoc committee of, 12, 13-14; first meeting of, 13; in charge of development, 15, 108; controls MC, 16, 108; assigns leasehold interest to new buyer, 17; buyer of A liable for SC arrears of previous, 17, 98; responsible for repairs, 22, 29; responsible for windows and doors, 23; responsible for glass, 23-24; cleans windows, 23-24; responsible for conduits and pipes, 24; refusal of, to carry out repairs, 24; right of, to connect to common installations, 24; right of, to quiet enjoyment, 24-25;

covenant of, to comply with House Rules, 25; freehold interest of, in PG, 26; limited powers of management of, 27, 108, 117; duty of, to dispose of non-domestic refuse, 29; BoD duty re breaches of rules by, 30; SC arrears, 30; breaches of House Rules by, 34; BoD need not consult, 34, 88, 115; dissatisfaction of, with MA, 35; sues D for mismanagement, 37, 98; dismissal of MA by, 38, 57, 77, 123; duty of, to pay rent, 42; duty of, to pay SC, 42, 74, 88; duty of, to repair and decorate, 42; duty of, to dispose of domestic waste, 42; car park usage by, 53; noise restrictions, 43-47; not to erect aerials and satellite, 48; duty of, not to hang clothes in A windows, 48; duty of, not to hang clothes on balconies, 48; domestic animals and birds in A, 48-49; duty of, not to display signposts and advertisements, 49-50; displays 'For Sale' and 'To Let' signs, 49-50; duty of, not to fit wooden floors, 50-51; duty of, not to let out part only of premises, 51, 67; duty of, to use A as single private residence, 51; use of balcony by, 51-52; duty of, not to make structural alterations, 52-53; duty of, not to decorate exterior of A, 52-53; prohibition of excessive weight, 53; prohibition of dangerous materials, 53; duty of, to allow access to A by MC, 54; not to cause nuisance, 55; indemnifies MC, 55-56; provides contact information to MA, 47, 59-60; duty of, not to run commercial activity in A, 51; influences BoD decisions at meetings, 54; legal proceedings against, for breach of L, 56; institutes legal proceedings against BoD, 57; replaces BoD at General Meeting, 57, 107, 108; secures own A, 62; informal meeting of, re car space marking, 67; requests details of lift contracts, 69; responsible for emergency callouts, 70; maintains own house in PG, 71; right of, to request budget details, 74, 90; informal meeting of, to discuss budget, 74, 77, 84; calls EGM to amend

AA, 77, 108, 122; refusal of, to pay SC without itemised budget, 77; specific costs relating to individual group of, 80; in ground floor A, cost of lifts, 80-81; reluctance of, to contribute to Sinking Fund, 84; short-term interest of, in A, 84; sells A, with inadequate Sinking Fund, 84; right of, to seek information about MA interest in contracts, 84-85; payment of SC by, 85; apportionment of SC among, 86; can't afford SC, 87; getting elected onto BoD, 88, 117; disagrees with annual budget, 88; challenge to budget by, 88; administration fees levied against, 91; threatens court proceedings against MA for 'SC collection policy', 92; removal of, as interested party from insurance policy, 93-96, 140; legal proceedings against, for SC arrears, 96-97; voting rights of, 98-99, 107, 108-110; 121; ; SC owed by, in first year, 100-101; right of, to receive annual accounts before AGM, 102; approves annual accounts at AGM, 102-103, 107; access of, to MC books of account, 103; should be aware of company structure, 106; duties and rights of, in AA, 107; entitled to copy of MAA, 107; right of, to attend General Meetings of MC, 107; right of, to be nominated for BoD, 108; right of, to call EGM, 108, 122; right of, to apply to Director of Corporate Enforcement and High Court, 108; no obligation of, to manage, 110; complaints by, to Director of Corporate Enforcement against BoD, 113; powers of, to remove directors at General Meeting, 116; becoming directors, the considerations of, 117-118; right of, to compel BoD to call EGM, 122; right of, to sue BoD and company secretary for MC strike-off, 125; suppression of minority rights of, 127; sues D for breach of contract for failing to transfer interests, 127; entitled to copy of insurance policy, 133; individual insurance cover, 137-138; decides on insurance policy excess, 139-140

Owner-landlord, 41, 147; duty of, to ensure tenants are aware of House Rules, 41, 129; eviction of tenants by, 46, 59; letting car space separately, 51; liable of, for administration fees for breaches by tenants, 56; MA contacts, re troublesome tenants, 58; renting out A, 129-130; liability of, for actions of tenants, 129; duty of, to act on complaints received by tenants, 130

Owner-occupier, 147

Ownership, of A, 1, 22-25; of freehold house, 2; of house in PG, 4, 130

Paint cans, disposal of, 43

Painting, common areas, 28; exterior of A by owner, 52; cost of, in private house, 82

Parking - see car parking

Parties, unruly and disruptive, 45-46

Payment of Service Charges - see Service Charges

Phones in lifts, cost of, in annual budget, 79

Pipes, 24; owners' right to connect to common installations, 24; in PG, 26

'Place of work', in Health & Safety regulations, 127; in PG, 130

Planning and Development Act 2000, 130

Planning permission, D's obligation to complete in accordance with, 11, 152; in Health & Safety file, 15; for erection of satellite dish, 48; for signs in A window, 50; for structural alteration to balcony, 53

Plants, on balcony, 52

Plaster cracks in apartment, 13

Playground areas, 25

Postage, cost of, in annual budget, 79

Power shower, use of, in A, 44

Premier Guarantee, 168

Premises, 22, 147; letting part only of, 51, 67; car space as part of, 65

Pressure and flow water test, by Local Authority, 64

Pressure equipment, engineering insurance for, 31

Private 'gated' development, freehold ownership of house in, 4, 19, 26, 130, 147-148; establishment of MC in, 4; membership of MC in, 4; easements in, 26; duties and obligations of BoD in, 39; MA fee in, 39; SC in, 39; owner maintains house in, 71; owners' duties in, 71-72; financial matters in, 103-104; as 'place of work' under Health & Safety regulations, 130; taking in charge of, 130-131; insurance matters in, 140; checklist when buying house in, 150-155

Problems in individual apartment, 13

Professional fees in annual budget, 79

Professional indemnity insurance, contractors, 30; MA, 114

Profit and loss account of Management Company, 121

Project management fees in annual budget, 79

Property owners' liability insurance - see also public liability insurance. 136-137; in annual budget, 79; in private house, 82

Proxy vote, 107

Public liability insurance - see also property owners' liability insurance. BoD duty to arrange, 31; in annual budget, 79; in PG, 19, 140

Qualified accounts, 102-103

Quasi ownership, 3

Quiet enjoyment, of leasehold house, 2

Quiet life, owner's right to, 24-25; MC covenant to ensure, 25; in PG, 26

Radiators in apartment, 24

Radio, noisy, 44

Rats, 28; vermin control in annual budget, 78

Refurbishment, in annual budget, 80

Refuse - see domestic and non-domestic refuse

Register of Companies, 102, 114, 120, 123, 124, 125, 132

Register of directors and secretaries, 119; BoD duty to maintain, 112, 116, 120; can be inspected by members of public, 119

Register of members, 107, 108; BoD duty to maintain, 112, 116, 120; can be inspected by members of public, 108

Registered office of Management Company, 106

Registrar of Companies - see Companies Office

Reinstatement valuation, in annual budget, 79, 83; 114; MA to keep under review, 134

Renting out apartment, 129-130

Renting, compared to owning, 1; renting land, 2

Repair and decorate A, owner's duty to, 42

Repairs, owners' responsibility for, 22; MC's responsibility for, 22; owner's refusal to carry out, 24; BoD obligations to, 28; BoD to obtain quotations for, 28; MA to appoint contractors for, 34; in annual budget, 78; included in Sinking Fund, 80; cost of, in private house, 82; in PG, 103-104; being ignored by BoD, 114

Requisitionists, calling EGM, 122

Requisitions on Title, 18, 148, 150; solicitor conducts, 6; BoD duty to furnish replies to, 30; query on Sinking Fund in, 84

Reserve Fund - see Sinking Fund

Reserved property, 25, 148

Residential Tenancies Act, 2004, 130

Residents' committee - see ad-hoc owners' committee.

Restoration, 125

Retained lands, 25, 148

Reversionary interest, 148-149; of leasehold house, 3; of apartment, 3, 105; D transfers, 14; owned by MC, 16

Rights-of-way - see easements

Roof, 25; structural problems with, 71; cost of, in private house, 82

Room hire in annual budget, 79

Rules introduced by MA, 33; in L, 41; breaches by tenants, 41

Safety Statement, 128, in PG, 130

Safety, Health & Welfare at Work Act, 2005, 128
Sales brochure, for development, 152
Satellite dishes, prohibition on erection, 48
Schedule of common installations, BoD to keep, 29
Second-hand apartment - see buying a second-hand apartment.
Security, systems, 9, 61-62; personnel, 62; owners' request to upgrade, 62; MA to deal with, 71; cost of, in initial budget, 75; cost of, in annual budget, 78
Self-managed developments, without MA, 31-32; emergency contacts in, 69; BoD chasing SC arrears in, 89; providing information to potential buyers in, 151
Service Charges, 149; payment on sale closing, 6; initial calculation of, 9, 76; pays for snagging, 11; withheld by dissatisfied owners, 12; arrears of previous owner on second-hand A, 17, 98; in Requisitions on Title, 18; BoD duty to recover arrears of, 30; BoD duty to calculate, 30; BoD duty to send invoice for, 30, 92; BoD duty to impose interest on arrears of, 30, 92; arrears of, in self-managed developments, 32; MA fees in, 32; owner's duty to pay, 42, 73-74, 88; administration fees to recover arrears of, 55; in PG, 72; BoD duty to levy, 74, 90; initial, budget figures for, 76; invoice for, should include breakdown of costings, 77, 90, 91-92; owner's refusal to pay, 77, 87-90; comparison with private house, 82; methods for payment of, 85, 90; apportionment of, 86; arrears, 91; 'collection policy', 91-97; in PG,104; voting rights of owners with arrears of, 98-99, 108, 121; credit forward of, in Years 1 and 2 of new development, 100-101; for unsold or unoccupied A's, 102; misappropriated by MA, 114; no procedures to chase arrears of, 114; 'collection policy' explanatory document sample, 164-166
Services, potential, available from MA, 158-160

Sewers, 24; owners' right to connect to common installations, 24
Share Certificate, 7, 17; BoD duty to issue, 30, 120
Sheets, shaking from A window, 48
Signatures on Management Company bank accounts, 100
Signpost, exhibiting in A window, 49-50
Singing, practicing in A, 44
Single private residence, A must be used for, 51
Sinking Fund, 83-84, 149; in Requisitions on Title, 18, 84; inadequate, in self-managed developments, 32; provision for lifts, 69; bank account for, 73; in annual budget, 73, 79; in initial budget, 75; BoD to decide level of, 76; inadequate, 84; control of account, 100; in PG, 103-104; inadequate, BoD liability for, 114; misappropriated by MA, 114
Small developments, MA fees in, 33
Smoke ventilation system, 28
Snag lists, responsibility of D, 9; developer slow to resolve, 10; not responsibility of MA, 10; owner must take action on, 11; in individual A's, 13
Solicitor for D, provides owner contact information, 60
Solicitor for MC, may receive Health & Safety file, 15; keep Title Deeds, 15; BoD can appoint, 30; check MA's contract, 38; deals with breaches of Lease, 56; sends notice to lending institution, 59; fees of, in annual budget, 79; checks 'SC collection policy', 91; writes to MA re access by BoD to MC books of account, 103; assistance of, required if owners take over BoD, 117
Solicitor for owner. Contact re snagging list, 11; collection of SC arrears from previous owner, 17, 98; Requisitions on Title, 18; contact re refusing to pay SC, 90; contact re suppression of minority rights, 110; investigates taking in charge in PG, 131
Sound insulation standards in A, 44
Special resolutions, at General Meetings of

MC, 123

Stairwells, 25

Standing order, payment of SC by, 85, 87

Stationery, cost of, in annual budget, 79

Stealing, insurance against, 136

Stereos, noisy, 44

Stolen vehicles in car park, 68

Storm, insurance against, 136

Strike-off, 114, 124-125; due to negligence of company secretary, 120; for not filing Annual Return, 123; in PG, 130

Structural alterations to A, 52-53; legal proceedings against owner for, 52

Structural problems, 71

Structural repairs in Sinking Fund, 83

Subscribers, 5, 149; voting rights at General Meetings, 109-110, 116, 121, 123, 126, 127

Subsidence, insurance against, 136

"Successful Apartment Living, Part 2" report, 128

Supplementary budget, 81, 83; BoD authority to introduce, 62, 71

Suppression of minority rights, 110, 127

Swimming pool, 25

Television aerials, prohibition on erection by occupier, 48

Television, noisy, 44

Tenants, 149; no long term interest, 41; letting bedroom to, 51; troublesome, 58, 129; eviction of, by owner-landlord, 59; contact information for, 61; actions of, in damp apartments, 70; complaints to owner-landlords from, 130

Title Deeds, D hands over to MC, 15

'To Let' signs, 49-50

Transfer of developer's interests, 8, 14-15; ad-hoc committee can put pressure on D, 14; D's refusal to transfer, 17

Troublesome neighbours, how to deal with, 57

Twenty-four hour emergency contact numbers, 69

Unoccupied apartments, SC for, 102

Unscheduled visits by MA, cost of, 79

Unsold apartments, SC for, 102

Useful contacts, 167-168

Valuation of buildings and equipment for insurance, 31

Vandalism, insurance against, 136

VAT, on administration fees, 55, 91; on MA's fee, 156

Vermin control, annual contract for, 78

Virtual freehold, 3

Visits by MA, 79

Voting, rights of owners, 98-99, 107, 108-109, 121; in AA, 107; proxy vote, 107; weight of votes, 109; subscribers' majority vote, 109-110, 116, 122, 123, 126, 127; in PG, 130

Walls, of A, 23; exterior walls, 25; in PG, 26

Washing machine, use of, in A, 44

Water leak, 24, cost of locating, insurance cover, 55, 136; emergency contacts re, 69; 70

Water pressure, poor, 64

Water pumps, plan for periodic maintenance of, 28; commissioning certificates for, 29; annual maintenance contract for, 78

Water tank, 24

Watering plants on balcony, 52

Weight of votes at General meetings, 109, 116, 122, 123, 126, 127

Windows, in A, 23; glass of, 23-24; cleaning of, 24; cleaning of, in common area 24, 28; owners' duty not to hang clothes in, 48; owners' duty not to exhibit signs in, 49; 'For Sale' / 'To Let' signs in, 49; cost of, in private house, 82

Wiring in apartment, 24

Wooden floors, 50-51; legal proceedings against owner for, 52